"Elizabeth has a addresses the most common conversation blocks: door slamming, yelling, and disconnection from the real world (iPads, phones) to name a few. This book provides a variety of strategies to help parents engage their teens in clear and meaningful conversations. I know that if this book existed when I was young, things would have been easier for me and my parents."

Theo Fleury
President, Fleury14 Ent. Inc

"Elizabeth has incredible experience having courageous conversations and isn't afraid to tackle the hard issues, which is what we need right now in our world. She brings a unique perspective with her work as a principal, as she has had to navigate hard conversations with students, parents, and teachers - sometimes all at once. This unique perspective she brings allows her to speak from an advantage to the topic of courageous conversations. Her book is timely for a world where our kids are needing connection more than ever."

Connie Jakab
Author of "Bring Them Closer"
Co-Founder of Certified Flourishing Coaching

"Elizabeth Bennett's professional background and extensive experience provides a profound masterpiece for initiating and guiding non-threatening conversations with teens. This book is a gift for the world of families, foster families, educators, social workers, law enforcement, parole officers, counselors and coaches in mastering conversations and relationship issues with teens."

Annette Stanwick, BScN
Speaker, Author, Freedom Facilitator & Coach
Best-selling & Award-winning Author of FORGIVENESS:
THE MYSTERY & MIRACLE

"I wish I would have had this book when I was raising teenagers. Now my children will be receiving copies to help with raising their teenagers. Thank you, Elizabeth, for this wonderful gift to assist parents and teens in their journey to improve their family dynamics for this and future generations; and for the many years of work and collaboration in ensuring the excellence of PMAST programs."

Brenda Christie, President
Peer Mediation and Skills Training

"Although decades in the making, this book is exceedingly timely. The post-Covid crisis is upon us as the effects of the past three years of the pandemic are increasingly showing up in families and children. That young people have been especially hard hit is well known to educators and helping professionals the world over. Although not referencing the vast body of knowledge on attachment theory and practice, Ms. Bennett's work is consistent with the principles and practice of this huge and fundamentally human area of scholarship. In her book, Ms. Bennett provides anti-dotes to our loss of community and connection endemic of our modern era made worse by Covid. Knowing her audience well, she has crafted a book that is both informative and instructional. There is much in this book that should be helpful to every parent facing the challenges of parenting at this challenging time."

Dr. Gregory F. Pickering,
Registered Psychologist

COURAGEOUS CONVERSATIONS

A Guide to Understand and Connect with Your
Teen

Elizabeth Bennett

Forward by Donna P. Dahl

Elizabeth Bennett Group
Calgary, AB
elizabeth_bennett@live.com

Elizabeth Bennett, author
Chelsey Devaud, cover art

ISBN 978-1-7782665-0-8   Paperback
ISBN 978-1-7782665-1-5   eBook

First Edition

The views expressed within this book are those of the author and are based upon her years of experience. The names and some situations have been changed to protect privacy. The author does not dispense medical advice or prescribe the use of any technique as a form of treatment for physical, emotional, psychological or medical problems without the advice of a physician either directly or indirectly. The intent of the author is only to offer information of a general nature to help you on your quest for emotional and spiritual well-being. The author and the publisher specifically disclaim liability, loss or risk, personal or otherwise, which is incurred as a consequence, directly or indirectly, of the use or application of any of the contents of this book.

"If you don't like what you got, why don't you change it?
If your world is all screwed up, rearrange it"
(Trooper – Raise a Little Hell)

To the child in all of us whose voice needed to be heard - let it be free now, so that you can change the world. . . today!

Table of Contents

Foreword

Teens. They are the adults of the future. The decisions they make will impact us for generations. Teens are at the crossroads of childhood and adulthood and they deserve the best in terms of mentorship, guidance, and support. Some teens make the transition smoothly; some find themselves in difficulty trying to sort out growing up.

From Chapter One, this book advocates for the teen who has been showing up in ways that need to be addressed. The behaviour being displayed is not acceptable and cannot be ignored. If punishment is the response of choice, that punishment is surely meant to address the negative behavior and encourage change for the better. Does this work? The underlying reasons for the behaviour may be invisible and totally unrelated to the event that just occurred.

It's easy to look at teen behaviour in terms of outward signals and make assumptions or read the clues incorrectly. A teen who is misunderstood or overlooked may become virtually invisible or make the list of repeat offenders within the tapestry of teenage life. Either way, these may be symptoms of deeper concerns.

Elizabeth Bennett invites you to peer into her world wherein she has had the opportunity to hone her skills at uncovering those all-too-often overlooked influences in a teen's life. She offers clues and conversation starters to help you get going on a better path. Her work clearly demonstrates her remarkable ability to connect with teens experiencing distress and to advocate on their behalf while gaining parental support.

While Elizabeth writes with the parent in mind, the big picture focus of this book is parents and their relationship with the school. Whether you are a foster parent, a teacher, a school administrator, a doctor, or a member of the police force, there is something here for you.

As a parent, you might argue that you are not a trained guidance counsellor, psychologist, or social worker and that you don't have the time or the skill to explore what else might be going on. Elizabeth gives you tools. She reminds us that the mindset, the mental health, and the life-long success of the child may depend upon your endeavours. Demonstrations of caring do matter.

Make no mistake, Elizabeth's real-life examples offer insight into how your upbringing and your modeling could impact your teen. You will be challenged to uncover the reason(s) behind the displays of their less-than-desirable behaviour. You will be challenged to find empathy for the overlooked causes, allow space for heartfelt kindness, and have a courageous conversation with the teen.

The school may be the setting of choice wherein the symptoms of something going wrong are acted out. Is acting out a matter for the delivery of a consequence such as punishment or is it a matter that deserves investigation? Her experience as a school administrator has taught her that schools and families need to work together. When they do not, the child (teen or preteen) may be caught in the middle when the child is the very person who deserves support and not alienation from all the vested parties including parents and teachers.

Her work does raise the question of where does belonging belong? Does it belong in the family? At school? On the team? Bullying is the very antithesis of belonging. Acting out may well be in the form of bullying. The setting may be on the playground, in a sports practice, on the bus, in a game or in a hallway. All this said is one thing; getting to the bottom of things is another.

I first met Elizabeth when I volunteered to be a speaker at her school in support of anti-bullying through the Peer Mediation and Skills Training (PMAST) organization. Her school hosted a PMAST event called Blue Friday to raise awareness about the incidence of bullying. The role of the speakers was to empower students with appropriate choices in response to bullying. I welcomed the opportunity to speak for personal reasons. The scars of bullying are invisible and the hurts that result linger long afterward. I know. I was bullied. If I helped one student break away from being a bully or being bullied, I am grateful to have played a part.

We were all teenagers once. Thinking back, were your teen years a time in your life you would prefer to remember or forget? Was it a time when you excelled at sports? Was it a time when you felt you didn't belong? Were you a straight arrow or did you find yourself warming a chair in the principal's office because you got singled out for something? Would an advocate for you have made a difference? Be it positive or negative, any baggage you carry from that critical time may still be present. This book will have you re-evaluating your beliefs and your practices of how you interpret and respond to your teen's misbehavior.

I applaud Elizabeth. She is a long hauler in the anti-bullying realm. She has long sought solutions for better outcomes for troubled teens. As an award-winning empowerment coach with a strong background in educational psychology and years of experience working with teens, I find Elizabeth's framework around having courageous conversations refreshing. It offers hope, but also action. It is certain to have you exploring ideas for communicating more effectively as you work respectfully toward improving the relationship with the teens in your care.

Donna P. Dahl, M. Ed.
Author, Speaker and Master Empowerment Coach
2022 Top Empowerment Coach List Worldwide
2020 Top 100 Canadian Professional List
2016 Woman of Inspiration
Donnapdahl.com

Introduction

I want to thank and acknowledge you for your interest in this topic. I will provide a variety of tools, strategies, and a few alternative perspectives as well as conversation starters that will serve to encourage and support you as you take on your courageous action to create a new relationship with your teen. There is no judgment, only ideas for you to try on and work through with your family.

> *COURAGE*: Mental or moral strength to venture, persevere, and withstand danger, fear, or difficulty as provided by Merriam-Webster Dictionary.

Bethany's Story

Bethany had been a cute child when she first showed up at our school doorstep. Unfortunately, she had severe medical concerns that took her out and away from school quite frequently as a younger student. She managed to keep up with most of her studies and her parents were as supportive as they could be, despite their own tumultuous relationship. Bethany was attentive in class and seemed to make friends easily as was demonstrated when she was laid up in hospital for a month due to a severe infection. The cards, flowers, and gifts flowed into her hospital room and left little space for her. Her mom would take pictures so that her classmates would know that Bethany was doing okay.

Moving into puberty a new attraction to boys and her tenacious spirit led to her getting into more trouble, in and out of school, when she reached jr. high. It was typical for Grade 8 girls to get tangled up in the hallway drama and, with the addition of cell phones, the stories that were shared turned into the mini-series of the decade. Needless to say, Bethany was entangled in that drama and in association with several unsavory guys well passed her age who enticed Bethany to get involved with some nasty behavior including drugs, alcohol, and sexual activity. Her parents came more frequently to the school to ask for assistance to make sure that she was attending, and to share information to help us keep Bethany under control at school. Time and time again she would not go home and would be on the street for days. Our school resource officer (SRO) became involved and, with the help of his local team, he was able to identify where Bethany would hang out when she wasn't at school. The administrative team at our school, including the counselor, created a plan and continued to support Bethany when she did attend school.

In one conversation that I had with Bethany and the counselor, Bethany shared that, "I met this guy in the group who was really nice to me, better than some of the others, and he told me he loved me." Bethany also shared that "my mom and dad are always arguing, and I don't want to be around that. It's safer in the place where I'm staying." The following time that the counselor and I met with the parents they were worried and relieved about where Bethany was staying; however, they had serious concerns about her safety. They said,

"We've noticed that her attitude and behavior have changed and it's worrisome for us and for her little sister, whom she adores. We are also concerned that she is not eating properly, and her health is beginning to deteriorate. She looks terrible. What can we do?" The parents also indicated that they had found a small amount of drugs in Bethany's clothes drawer. "These could really kill her because of all of the medication that she is taking for her illness," Bethany's mom said.

We had a conversation with the police officers who picked up Bethany and brought her to school one morning when they were on patrol in the neighborhood. As it turned out, Bethany did have a small amount of cocaine in her possession. The police were informed and appropriate measures were taken.

Between the hospital, the so-called hang-out house, and occasionally landing at home, arrangements had finally been made with the assistance of the community outreach paediatric team associated with our school district, who made a recommendation for a redirection for Bethany to be placed in a locked down treatment facility to support her as she recovered. Shortly after her entry into the facility, Bethany quickly found eager participants to the antics she created. Most of the clients within the facility were there for their own recovery from a variety of drug related situations in which they had participated. We all agreed that it was the best placement for her, to get her away from the 'hang-out house' and the temptation of drugs and sexual activity that she had become accustomed to while out on the street. I met with Bethany and the social worker at the facility to discuss the possibility of day treatment and social outings as Bethany demonstrated good behavior, and a transition back into the community. The social worker also visited with us at the school on a few occasions to keep us up to date with Bethany's progress.

Several weeks had passed and Bethany had been quickly discharged from the facility after her attempted plot. Bethany had created a little scenario where she traded her so-called drugs. In this case it had been sugar that she tried to sell to a few other clients of the facility.
Because they frowned upon that type of activity Bethany was quickly discharged, never to return to the facility. She came back to school with her mother a few days after her release and we met to figure out our next plan of action regarding Bethany returning to school.

Bethany made it clear that she was going to do her best to re-engage with her classes and try hard to complete work. She asked for extra assistance within the classes that she attended and was also agreeable to help after school with other students and teachers who were willing to support her efforts. That lasted for about a month and then she found her way back on the street to the 'hang-out house'. This time though, the police were able to contact the actual homeowner, have the place shut down, and arrest a few of the 'group leaders' for illegal drug activity and inappropriate participation with minors. Unfortunately, they just found another location to hang out.

In late summer I received a call from our school counselor telling me that Bethany's mom had called her and explained that Bethany had passed away. It was so difficult to accept that she was gone. Bethany was a very bright young woman who had so much potential, and it was taken from her and her family so young in her life.

This didn't have to happen to Bethany. This is one of the reasons why you need to have Courageous Conversations with your teen.

Do you feel that you are losing connection with your child?

Are chaos and crises driving your family apart?

Is your kid's behavior driving you crazy?

These are just a few of the many questions and areas that will be addressed in this book.

Give yourself permission to be vulnerable with yourself and your child. Perhaps you'll need to find extra patience that you perhaps misplaced or have lost somewhere, it's going to be important.

In all likelihood this wasn't an overnight transition from a great relationship to where it is at the moment, and it also won't be an overnight solution. Be patient with yourself. You can't wait any longer; your teen is important, likely the most important person in your life. Your child is dying for you to take the first step.

In my 35 years of experience in teaching and as a school principal it has been my passion and my focus to understand the inherent aspects of relationships; what makes lasting ones, why there is conflict, what purpose does it serve, and how can we make things better in people's lives. One of the things I've heard frequently is that raising a child is hard work. It's true, even from the school point of view. I have also heard an African saying that "it takes a village to raise a child." This is where we can shift how things work from home as well as school. When we work together as the village we can help to support each other, understand each other's perspectives, needs, wants, and desires and work together to come up with the best plan of action. This can include tackling issues from different perspectives, exchanging information to keep everyone informed (ex: noticing different behaviors in different environments, attitude changes, etc.). As challenging as it may be, working together can help to shed light on what could be happening at school or at home so that, when possible, the school can help to support the family or the child directly.

When I was a child, I was alone, lonely, and not really truly connected with my parents. It was not the best home environment and I always wished for someone to talk to. My parents both worked full time and I was the responsible only child. I was a pleaser so as not to get into trouble, although arguments with my dad did happen quite frequently, while my mother tried to be the peacemaker. In elementary school I was a tomboy and engaged in many of the playground activities with all of the other kids as well as when we played in the community. In high school such was not the case. I was basically the third in each of the 'best friend' partners and I was also a target of harassment and bullying. Even back then I wanted to find a way to have things be different, but at that point I didn't really know how. I just knew there had to be a better way, and I wasn't going to let all of that ruin my life.

My initial passion for writing this book was to be "the person" who was going to provide the magic bullet for ending bullying while helping to create safe and caring lives and changing the world. What I soon discovered through my own personal life challenges, which started in early childhood, accompanied by my desire to make a difference in the lives of students and possibly their families, was the reality that there wasn't some magic bullet that was going to make a difference, erase suffering or make everything rosy. Rather it was the challenges, struggles, and celebrations that have been shared with me, as well as those that I experienced throughout the years, that made me realize the true nature of breaking through the underlying anxiety, depression, social isolation, bullying issues, mental health concerns and so on, comes down to the basic need for relationship, connection, and community.

You see, if we've lost our way with our kids and each other it becomes very challenging to work through the issues or concerns, and the result is often the loss of connection.

> *If we have the courage to share, to talk with each other and really be there, the walls begin to crumble, the light starts to break through the cracks which brighten the path, and we begin to create new relationships with each other.* Elizabeth Bennett

When I first started this book, almost 25 years ago, I was involved with several community agencies who helped support a focus I had on stopping bullying in my school. I wanted to have every child, at that time specifically our Grade 7 students, to feel safe, feel empowered, have resilience, and be change makers in the world. However, even with those amazing full day leadership 'group dynamics' workshops, further teaching, and follow up within that school year and the next, implementing changes that the students suggested, and individual restoration with each other, it still didn't seem to be enough. The program was successful in concept, but we knew that in order to achieve lasting impact this needed to be a family and community-wide initiative, not merely something we implemented within the school, so we shared it with the town council. After much discussion at several town council meetings, it was decided to create a mandate for the town to "strive to be a bully free community." The program was also presented to the local school district and the Restorative Justice Committee, and was met with overwhelming support and engagement.

As we all know, when leadership changes, either within the school or within the town, and the authorities' focus shifts to other priorities programs sometimes drop away, they are no longer funded or the 'bright shiny' of the moment fades away or disappears. Unfortunately, that happened with the program and the town focus. However, the burning desire in my heart to find a solution was still raging and I knew that I wanted to do something about it. Family disconnects continued to mount, children began to contemplate taking their lives, and I didn't want that to happen to any more children.

I continued my quest to understand the dynamics of relationship, and in my position as a teacher and an administrator I asked students for their opinions. I invited their contributions and their experiences as well as having that same opportunity during discussions with parents. Patterns began to emerge with both the responses from parents as well as those from students:

TEEN'S VIEWPOINT	PARENT'S VIEWPOINT
They don't really understand what it's like out there for me	My child doesn't understand me
The peer pressure is so hard and heavy	The stress of home and work
We always get into arguments	We always get into arguments
Why don't they listen or hear me	They don't listen or hear me
Why doesn't my opinion count?	My opinion is not valued

Please ask me different questions "I'm not always fine . . ."	Please ask me how I'm doing
It's easier to be on my phone, people see me and listen to me	My phone helps distract me
I can't talk to my parents	I can't connect with my teen
I don't know who they are anymore	I don't know who they are anymore
Is it me, or are they changing?	Is it me, or are they changing?
What's with the attitude and behavior?	Their attitude and behavior are intolerable
All we do is yell and scream	All we do is yell and scream

I continued to engage in reading more books and articles as well as attending professional development programs so that I could enhance my 'tool kit' and share my learnings with others including teachers, students, parents, and community agencies. Although these learnings were important and valuable for student success and achievement, I saw yet another missing link or rather a 'missing connection'. Even with presentations and courses, workshops and so on, including educational learning experiences for students, oftentimes these programs were not necessarily available or supported with participation by parents.

The consequence of this was that the only time parents became aware of any of these tools was if they met directly with me or my staff to discuss strategies, or if their teen shared their learning with them. This resulted in denial or lack of opportunities to help support their children with the concepts that were provided through participation in these programs at school.

Even if students were to share what they learned with their parents, they wouldn't necessarily be able to clearly explain or provide examples of their learning. Also, if there wasn't a well-defined understanding or engagement by the parents to model, then the disconnect soon became bigger. Many programs were unable to achieve a sustainable component in or out of school. In addition, unless the teachers continually emphasized the key learning points from the presentation, there wasn't much to support the student follow-through or achieve real implementation of their own learning. In other words, if they didn't feel supported and it was treated as a "one off" program, the tangible learnings were replaced with wishes and dreams of hope rather than continuous growth or pursuit of their personal passion.

Here's where this book comes into play; I am going to support you on your journey by providing you with questions, reflections, and stories that will help you to understand what could very well be happening with your young person. I've had the good fortune and have been blessed with sharing conversations with students as well as many parents. My desire is that the lessons I've learned, and am now sharing with you, will serve as a conduit to creating strong and meaningful relationships between you and your child(ren).

As I mentioned before, you are not alone on this journey! Many families are embarking on this challenge. This is meant to be a breakthrough from fear to COURAGE for you and your teen. To actually step into having Courageous Conversations with your teen. It's TIME to CONNECT!

Chapter 1
From Chaos to Courageous Conversation

"With all the stuff that happens in a day, how do you respond?"

Picture this: you've hit the snooze button two or three times, you finally look at the time and now you sit up with a start, throw the covers back, and quickly jump out of bed. "Oh my God, we're late!" Getting dressed, you remember that you were supposed to get gas last night and thought you would do that this morning because you know you don't have enough gas in the car to get to the corner, let alone to work. "Holy shit!" you say to yourself out loud.

Now let's add a teenager or two into the mix! You hustle into their rooms and wake them up because you know they don't move as fast as the speed of light when you want them to do something.

Can you relate to this scenario? Maybe this has never happened to you personally, but let's stop and think about it for a minute. As challenging as it has been to get it all together for you, your child doesn't have the skills that you have to get the day started.

Let's imagine that inside of them is a simmering pot. Having been abruptly woken up from a sound sleep, that probably just started a few hours ago because of their quiet obsession with social media and games, they are trying to get up.

You are yelling at them because again, we know that getting up before noon is quite a challenge for most youth! They hear "You're not wearing that, are you?" Then they are nagged about eating breakfast "You know it's the most important meal of the day," comes from some voice in the kitchen. While stuffing food into their faces, they might manage to have you sign their field trip form and do whatever things that it takes for them to get out the door and maybe make it onto the bus on time.

How do you suppose that relationship is going for you and your child so far? Here's a place that you might consider reflecting upon. How could that situation have been handled differently? A suggestion that you could provide would be that all of you meet at the end of the day and say that it didn't go as well as we all had hoped, so let's talk about it. Admit that yelling doesn't help, and offer, "think about how we could make that different for tomorrow. Let's talk about it when we get home tonight." When you chat later that evening, you could say, "I'm sorry that we slept in . . . it sure did make the start of our day quite frantic." Then ask, "What suggestions can you think of to help make things work, even when we are rushed? How can we all help to contribute to making the mornings work better?"

Can you see how different the outcome would be rather than with yelling? The elements of reflection and engagement begin to help everyone to understand their contribution and move forward in a more positive way.

Let's carry on and look at the scenario possibly bubbling up at school:

On the bus, stupid things happen. Kids are yelling at each other; someone grabs another kid's hat and throws it a few seats away. Kids are teasing and bragging to each other about something or other, which your teen doesn't typically get involved with during the ride to school. However, in their heightened state, the hat comes sailing through the air, and wouldn't you know it, the brim of the hat smacks your kid on the side of the head. Your teen tosses the hat away while saying some rude, crude and socially unacceptable comment which now gets reported to the office by the bus driver.

So now at school that simmering pot is getting close to the bubbling and boiling stage. Your child eventually gets to their locker, bumped and pushed in the crowded hallway, as they grab their stuff and make their way to class.

Are you still with me?

Walking into class, being reminded about a test or assignment that is coming up, they are asked about their homework. They are trying to find a good seat; however, the seating has been rearranged, or some other tiny thing that you can't even imagine, can be the very thing that sets them off. Thoughts go racing through their mind that the teacher doesn't care because all the teacher is worried about is getting the work done, collecting papers, permission forms, assignments or just getting them to sit down. The teacher is trying to get the students' attention to get the day started, meanwhile it sounds like the teacher is yelling at them, and they've just been yelled at by folks at home. So now they are not much interested in engaging in anything that the teacher has to say or wants them to do. That's part of the challenge. Then there's the EXPLOSION!

Not even 20 minutes after the bell and Jamie is in my office. "Good morning Jamie, what's up?"

"Teacher kicked me out of class."

"Come on in, let's talk about it." I motion to where the chairs are, and I sit down at my desk. Pacing back and forth, steam blowing out of his ears, Jamie says in a raised voice,

"The classroom tables and chairs were moved around, and she made me sit beside this kid who always bullies me. He always says stuff under his breath when no one else is around or listening. He did it again today! I'M SICK OF IT! So I grabbed him and tried to punch him and then the desk flipped. . . and then she kicked me out. She didn't even know what happened. I was the only one who had to leave. I kicked the garbage can and slammed the door on my way out of the classroom. I was pissed!"

Jamie, still looking red in the face and escalated, continued to pace. I gave a bit of space for silence then I inquired with a quiet, compassionate voice, "Did anything else happen?"

23

He reached for the chair, sat down, leaning forward with elbows on his knees, he put his head in his hands. Mumbling, he said, "My mom kept yelling at me to get up 'cause we got up late. She always complains about what I wear and sometimes makes me take it off and put on something else. She made that dumb comment about breakfast, you know, it's the best for you, whatever." Lifting his head he looked right at me and said defiantly, "I HATE breakfast! And then I was late for practice, and the coach made me run extra laps and do 50 push-ups before I could play. He hates it when we are late. The bus driver probably gave you guys a note because I saw him writing something when I was leaving the bus. Because I got hit in the head with somebody's stupid hat, and I yelled at the kids in the back. He told me that I swore at them." Sitting back in his chair, he looked defeated. "And now my mother's going to kill me."

How do you suppose that relationship is going with that teacher and your child? How do you think your teen feels about how things are going?

As we learn more about brain chemistry and the parts of the brain, we know that pre-teens and teens don't often have the skills and strategies necessary to be able to manage to keep a lid on what's going on in their life. The best part is that we know several strategies necessary, and we know for sure that it starts with a Courageous Conversation. We wonder why kids explode on the playground or in the classroom. It's usually because, as I mentioned, they don't have the skills, experience, or the wherewithal to have the correct response or to react appropriately when they have just been yelled at by someone who is supposed to love them. They get pushed and shoved in the hallway, someone looked at them funny, or something happened in a game on the playground that didn't go their way and they react poorly. This is where we come in as parents, educators, administrators, community members, and coaches to model a different type of response or action. It's worthy of reflection; you need to be there to help them reflect and provide alternative choices so that they begin to see how they react won't always solve their problems. It comes down to 'teaching and learning' for both of you. Will it always be a winning conversation? Not necessarily; however, it will be the start of something new. And it all starts with you and how you respond.

How do You Show up for Them and How do You Respond?

The intent is for you to understand that these types of conversations are not simply a onetime 'sit-down and solve the problem quickly' with your young person. They require ongoing follow-up and check-ins to ensure the information and feelings shared are kept sacred, respected, and dignified.

Let's look back on the morning story. Remember, it's you who gets up late with your family. After all of that morning chaos in your house, you had to get gas, get the little ones to day care and you got to work late. You are in a hurry to get on with your day, trying to get back on track and you are generally capable of putting the 'frantic' behind you . . . or so you think. You've missed having your coffee or other beverage that helps you get energized, the extra time that you usually take to get things organized, the few minutes that you might chat with your colleagues, none of that happened today. So you are scrambling a bit, trying to regroup, and perhaps you are looking at your plan and having to make some quick changes. At this point you are hardly into your day when you get a call from Jamie's school principal saying that he has been suspended from school for fighting. You call your partner, inform them of the situation and ask them to pick up Jamie. "We'll talk when we get home!"

Trying to refocus, you're a little rattled and in walks a colleague with a report that you both had been working on for the presentation this afternoon, and she says that there seems to be a part missing. You quickly snap back at her and realize what you have done. Apologizing, you explain that the morning didn't go quite as well as planned and everyone was a bit frazzled,

"I just got a call from my son's school saying that he's been suspended. That won't sit particularly well with my partner. Anyway, I'm sorry, let's have a look and see about the missing parts, I may still have them here." In the middle of your presentation, the internet goes down. How are you responding?

The day progresses and you finally leave your office, a bit drained, grateful for drive home. You get a chance to decompress as you sit in traffic in an effort to get home before the late news. You turn on the radio to hear P!nk singing "I've had a shhhhdy day, you've had a shhhhhdy day" and you begin to laugh out loud.

As you arrive home you are greeted by the dog, who makes you smile, and you breathe deeply and sigh as you close the front door. The silence is deafening. You look around and see your partner in the office and your child sprawled on the couch with a pillow over his head. You kick off your shoes, go to the office and share a kiss, and then return to the living room as you approach the couch you say, "Hi honey, so tell me about your day," as you sit beside him. Leaving a space for silence you eventually say,

"I can well imagine that it was likely as rocky as mine. I almost bit off Terry's head today when she gave me back the report that we had been working on and told me that a piece was missing. Luckily, I had in on my computer, and we were able to finish it on time for our meeting. Then the internet went down, thankfully we were able to complete our meeting with a conference call. Oh, what a day! I spoke briefly with your principal who told me you had a fight in your class. We had such a frantic start to our day, I can only imagine that it might have had an impact on you. So, tell me what happened."

A few days later when Jamie returned to class after the suspension, the teacher quietly asked to speak with Jamie when the class was over.

"Hey, I'm glad you're back." The teacher asked, "What happened the other day that got you so riled and made you want to fight? That's not normally like you." Jamie explained to the teacher about waking up late, the incident on the bus and the desks being switched around, the kid that always bugs him that he hit, and being late for practice.

"And then my dad had to come and pick me up. We had a long talk about how to handle stuff. I'm grounded, no video games, no cell, no activities for this week. I get it, I shouldn't have done it."

With a shocked look on her face, the teacher exclaimed "Wow! That's a lot of stuff! Thanks for telling me, I'm sorry that all of that happened to you. Listen Jamie, why don't you meet me after school for a bit so that I can help you catch up with work that you missed. Let me know if that can work and we can also talk about a new seating arrangement."

It has been through the wisdom of the years, during my own conversations with students, parents, teachers, and in other areas of my personal life, that I have come to realize that there really is a format to listening. I've developed these dedicated listening strategies that are interwoven so that they become seamless when practiced, and it allows space to be curiously engaged and focused solely on the conversation that is being had with your loved one.

Principles of Courageous Conversation

From the scenario that you have just read, let's break it down so that you can get ideas for engaging in conversation that don't end up as a yelling match.

Principle # 1: Find Out What's Really Going On

It's becoming increasingly more important to change our focus when dealing with young people and teens when trying to be supportive and building a relationship with them. We need to take the time to find out by inquiring and engaging in conversation about what may have happened to them, rather than starting a conversation with "What's wrong with you?" which, in my experience, has been the default focus. That question has negative connotations and is quite judgmental, so it often leads to silence from the very person you are hoping to support. When your tone is different, and the words you use are less confrontational, it becomes a more approachable situation for your teen to respond. Keep in mind that it will take a while, a few conversations perhaps, for them to answer, particularly when that hasn't been your most positive self showing up and asking the question or being curiously engaged.

Principle #2: Reframing Your Behavior

This requires a shift in effort for you, to being much more curious in engagement with an open mind as opposed to expecting an answer when you already have the solution prepared in your head or on the tip of your tongue, ready to spew out at your child. These automated-response experiences can come from many sources, and not only does it demonstrate that you, as the parent, are not listening to your child, but these types of responses are a shock to their system. Often, depending on the child's age when these experiences occurred, they would not likely have the developed skills and coping strategies with which to deal appropriately.

Powerful and trusting relationships with family members, coaches, teachers, counselors can be the saving grace for students or children who have faced one or more of these adverse experiences. One of the major concerns when children are of school age is they may not recognize that not every other person whom they encounter is like their aggressor.

Now, here's where the challenging parts come into play for the young person or teen. When they experience guilt, shame, grief or loss, resentment, and or trust issues, often they will have shared that they don't feel safe, or that they don't have anyone whom they can trust. We'll break this down a little further in Chapter 6 when we do a deep dive into holding space for strong emotions, as each of these feelings are quite complex when they are all muddled up in a child's head and heart.

Are You Really Listening?

Do you ever notice that you try to do several things at the same time because you think it will save time, only to find out that you make mistakes or become so scattered that nothing ends up being done well? This often happens when you say you are listening to your teen at the same time as you are watching a show or scrolling through "likes" on your personally owned cellular device. How often has that happened with you and to you? Well, it's time to practice putting the cell phone down, with the ringer off and re-engaging in conversation with your teen. They are wanting to do the same thing, deep inside, but would prefer to disengage in conversation and get lost in the world of online communication. I believe that some of you might be nodding your head in agreement and saying to yourself "but it was important," or some other thought that justified your choice of actions of staying connected to your device rather than stopping what you are doing. But remember, there is nothing more important than your child in this moment.

What do you think would happen if you all agreed to set aside some *intentional time* to have a real-life conversation with your teen? Don't expect the answers or the conversation to be what you want it to sound like, rather, seek to *understand first* what your teen might be saying or not saying, before attempting to be understood. Most of us don't listen with the intent to understand, we listen with the intent to reply. Stay with listening, try not to give your own opinion when they are speaking. Remember to check in with them to see if they want you to answer, to solve the dilemma, or to just listen. Asking is ok, it gives your teen the sense of value in themselves and that you really want to listen to what they have to say.

Let me introduce you to strategies and skills that will help you create a better space for connection.

Five Strategies of Dedicated Listening

Understanding vs Judgment

Looking beyond the behavior and be curiously engaged

Your child comes raging in the door after school, slams the door, throws the backpack against the wall and stomps up to their room without even a 'hello'. You'll want to ask yourself the question: What's going on that is creating this behavior?

Reflect for yourself on what has been occurring around your home or with your family dynamics and relationships. There could be clues there that have not been fully explored. What have you noticed that could be behind the behavior? Have there been any major changes that could impact your teen's mood or attitude? Here's where seeking clarity and understanding by being curiously engaged comes into play. If you have an attitude or opinion for everything that they are sharing with you, that will quickly shut the door on any opportunity to assist them in moving through their challenge or dilemma. Begin by starting the conversation, while being careful about your tone. Inquire about the situation that has just occurred.

"I noticed that you didn't even say 'hi' when you came in, what's going on?" Be sure to soften the tone as there was heat in that entry into the house. Use silence to allow your child time to process an answer. Don't rush them, it may take a bit to reduce the emotional upheaval that currently exists. "Hey, so tell me what's happening these days? What's been going on for you? I've noticed that you have been (angry, sad, mad, grumpy, disengaged, any number of other emotions that you might have noticed) lately, tell me what's going on?" This can be a sentence starter for another conversation at a later date, considering that you are attempting to keep the situation calm during this conversation.

It's important to keep the questions open ended, so that you don't get caught up in the 'yes or no' answers that your teen will throw your way. If you get the 'yes or no' answers only, without any explanation, it will not allow for any further conversation and will frustrate both of you. The idea is that you want their viewpoint on what might be bothering them. This could include, and is not limited to, what is in their way that they can't see clearly, or that they are feeling trapped and can't see beyond themselves. Allow the response to be theirs, not what you want to hear. It is important to stay focused with the idea about understanding your teen, versus your judgment on what they are saying. Be welcoming and inviting so that they feel safe in the space of 'dedicated listening'. Trust is paramount to your teen, and it is also going to take some time to have it become established with you, especially if calm, Courageous Conversations have not normally been your style of communication.

Emotions are complex - no judgment for showing emotions

Understanding that your teen's emotions are not yet fully developed is important to keep in mind. They will likely not be able to clearly or fully describe their emotions. This would be a good time to carefully select a few examples and test the waters of how they respond. Ask them to identify a location in their body that is holding the feelings that are happening within them. Have your child explain how it feels for them, "What do you suppose is going on that is making you feel that way? How does it show up in your body? Where do you feel the most discomfort or feeling of pain?" You as the parent can add to the conversation by mentioning to your child, "providing some details for me will help me to understand a bit better about how you are doing. I realize that it is difficult to explain, but give it a try, I'm listening."

"It's tight in my chest."

"It feels like I have knots in my stomach."

Silence is golden at this point. Give them a chance to process your question while they scan for their feelings and determine whether they can provide an answer. Don't be surprised if they say "I don't know" initially. It's likely that they haven't been asked that question before and haven't given it any definitive thought as to what it really feels like. They just know that they feel discomfort.

It is often assumed that since your child is a certain age they should show it, act it, and be it; however, it is not that easy for them to always show up how you imagine they should. This is a growing and developing stage. It's important to understand that peer and personal pressure weighs heavily on your teen. 'What people think' has way more influence on your child than you think. For them it is beyond rational thinking, and it may not be 'cool' to express emotions or act in certain ways, particularly around their peers. These unexpressed feelings oftentimes lead to anxiety, fear, and emotional withdrawal, based on what your teen imagines their friends will say or how they will react if emotions are demonstrated in the peer group.

Behavior is a form of communication

What has your teen been trying to tell you? "Please hear what I'm not saying!"

Is help on the way for your teen or is criticism and berating what they expect to hear from you? Teens will often respond with thoughts in their head, "I push you away and I pull you toward me. I know that you will leave, see, I told you so." When you stomp out of the room, frustrated because your teen won't share with you what is going on with them. Perhaps they haven't quite figured it out yet and you are too upset to wait for them to discuss it with you.

"What's the point, you don't listen anyway!" Your teen may not say this out loud, but they certainly are thinking it. That thought has been shared with me numerous times by many teens.

"You always think that you have the (right one) or that yours is the only answer. It's not always how you think. You wouldn't understand anyway."

"I'm afraid you won't love me anymore."

"I don't know how to tell you."

Their insecurity can demonstrate itself through anger, like throwing their backpack, creating a fuss in their class, not completing their work and not caring. It could also be in their response to a simple question that you have asked, and they begin chewing your face off when they speak to you. A very common response is saying "fine" or "good" when it's really not. Avoiding or evading conversation with you, hiding in their room, not engaging with the rest of the family. These are also illustrations of communication, albeit not the greatest forms of connection.

This is where your investigative skills get to be sharpened.

Finding FLOW

Allow your teen to guide the conversation

We often talk too much as adults, we rationalize or react before we know what is really going on. We often don't give children the opportunity to really express what is going on for them. The underlying particulars of your teen's problem or concern often are not evident at first. They may start with some story that you don't believe to be important; keep listening. Their sentences often stop and start with whatever they are trying to express, not quite knowing how to fully express the issue or concern. Let them share the story, however it comes out from them. Try to read between the lines for other clues, but don't overthink or overreact, give them time to explain.

Timing is everything. Don't try to interrupt the flow of their story unless there is a definite pause or long silence. Then you can ask questions for clarity. Don't assume you know what they are saying because if you don't really know and you pretend that you do, it will bite you in the ass. The clarity and weaving in of paraphrasing, in other words saying some of their words back to them, will provide an opportunity to expand on your Courageous Conversation, and confirm if you are on the right track. This also helps your teen to know that you are actually listening and really understanding them.

You could say something like "Just so I'm clear, when you said _____ is that what you really meant?" If you assume rather than asking, it could easily shut down the conversation because your teen will think you weren't even really listening. Remember the trust component, it's massive for your teen.

Acknowledge your teen for their contribution to the conversation

Authentically acknowledge, "This must have been really difficult for you to share."

"I'm amazed at your courage, thank you for sharing this with me."

"I can't imagine what this must have been like for you carrying this for so long."

Don't rush the conversation, use some new sentence starters or questions to get and keep the ball rolling:

"Tell me more about this _____,"

"How do you suppose they feel when you. . . ?"

"What are you hearing out there?" Examples: these could be pressures, things that other people are saying, the weight of decisions to be made as in the next school year, dating, college, activities, career, just to name a few.

"What do you think people are saying? What gives you that impression?"

"What would you like to do about it? How important is it to you?"

"Will it be important a few years from now?"

Be careful not to make light of these questions.

Intentional Time

Remove distractions

You may find it challenging to turn off your cellular device. Seriously, nothing is more important than your own child! Turn off the TV, computer, iPad, video games, perhaps even your music. I think you get the picture, no pun intendedJ Clear your calendar of all other tasks, appointments, and meetings. This is IMPORTANT TIME! Schedule this time in your calendar and don't diminish it either with your colleagues, friends or family members. This is critical. Remember the 'trust factor'? Your teen is listening and watching your every move as they 'test the waters' of real connection with you, and you with them.

Intentional focus "be with them"

It really means that you are dedicated to focusing, both with your ears and with your eyes, in your Courageous Conversation with your teen. It's awkward and uncomfortable at first if you are not used to this type of connection, but stay with it. You need your teen to know that you are just with them, and nothing else is important. It's vulnerable, scary and *"What if I don't do it right?"* you say to yourself. Tell your teen "This is a learning and growing experience for me too." Ask them to give you a break as you work through the discomfort. Just a gentle reminder to be very careful with your tone and level of frustration. It can sometimes catch you by surprise as you are trying to engage in conversation and there is a stall or a non-responsive attitude. It takes time and you are committed now. Set the time without an ulterior motive. "I missed my golf game for this, so let's have it!" won't cut it with your teen. This is about patience; yours more specifically. Keep in mind that this conversation may not happen the first time, particularly if you haven't made it a point of trying this before now. It's your courage to hang in there that will make the biggest difference in your relationship with your teen. You've got this!

NO JUDGEMENT here, just making you aware that you might consider this a waste of time. Somewhere in your mind perhaps you have this thought going on, be honest with yourself. It happens and this will be an opportunity for you to work through it. Families have shared that this is difficult at first; however, both parents and teens have appreciated the tenacity that it took to stay the course.

Empower your relationship by coming alongside

Acknowledge that this will be somewhat uncomfortable, uneasy, and at the same time, have some fun around it. Perhaps you haven't been out with your teen before, just the two of you. Say it to them, laugh about it and make it a big deal. It should be fun, this is your child, for goodness sakes. Also, make it a regular date, as you do with your other commitments, it's really worth the effort. Put it in your calendar and don't diminish it!

Understand First, Speak Second

Ask about your role

When your teen begins to share something with you or asks to chat with you, *ask about your role*. "Would you just like me to listen? Are you looking for advice? It's okay if you don't know yet, I'll listen and then we can discuss it later. Can that work for you?"

If they aren't sure, just acknowledge it and let them carry on with the conversation.

Share solutions only if requested

Be prepared to 'hold your tongue' and try to refrain from providing your own feedback and not eagerly jumping into the conversation. Just a reminder, this is about listening. It's very challenging, stay with it!

Provide alternative perspectives

It becomes very easy for us as adults to jump into the conversation with both feet and to use our own experiences as the example when trying to explain something to a teen. "When I was your age." You've likely heard that one in your own lifetime and have probably used it as well. Try to limit your own sharing of experiences; rather, give your teen examples of their friends or situations that they can relate to in a teen context. Parent says, "What gives you that idea? What do you think your friend Daniel would say about that?" The teen then must reflect on how their friend would react to a particular situation, and it becomes a more relatable suggestion or idea to use in the conversation. Often, when parents share their life experiences the teen does not understand or retain the message behind the share, they take on the attitude of the parental experience and then use it as their own. Remember when you told me Daniel's story? It made me laugh when he said,

"My dad skipped school many times in Grade 7, so I think it's okay for me to do it too, because I'm already smart. And besides, he owns a company and is doing really well." Daniel likely doesn't quite know the complexity or the background of the story that his parent had shared. Perhaps the parent received a punishment or a suspension for his behavior and conveniently left that part out when telling Daniel the story. Probably for good reason, however, it shifts from the importance of the conversation between parent and teen when extreme examples are used to illustrate a point.

Provide opportunities for your teen to see and discuss alternative sides of the story, illustrating the impact that each perspective could have. You could start the conversation with, "So, let's say you want to experiment with drugs, (*or sleep with your partner in their home or in ours, or you want to stay out later than your regular curfew time, or ask someone on a date, or break up with someone on a text*), how would you receive the information?" Be aware that your teen might respond with "I wouldn't care" or "It wouldn't bother me." This would be a great time to have your teen explain why they don't care, or why it wouldn't bother them, for clarity's sake. Oftentimes this is the resistance piece to acknowledging their own feelings and the fear of how it would be if that situation occurred or really happened to them. Teens don't necessarily want to deal with decision making and the emotions that get attached to the incident. They would rather ignore and move on so as not to 'feel' because it hurts too much, and they at some point have felt the hurt, and it has been too difficult.

You want them to really contemplate how decisions have an impact, whether we act or we don't, there is always going to be an impact. It gives your teen an indication of how to think through the whole scenario. It may take time to process, so be certain to give the time and the silence that your teen needs to come up with their response. Inquiry usually arises from this part of the conversation. However, it's important that every effort be made to keep your emotions out of the Courageous Conversation, by helping to keep the calm, and not being the only one to have 'the' answer. Listening for understanding is KEY!

Reflective Engagement

Choose to let go of your answers or solutions

    This can be particularly difficult for you as a parent or caregiver when all you want to do is "solve the problem" for your teen, usually out of care and love. Allow them the opportunity to work through it with you. This is a time of expansion of thought for both of you. Letting go provides you more space to be 'dedicated in your listening' to what your teen is saying, not what you want to say in response.

Use a few of your teen's own words to ask a question or reiterate what they are saying.

    "When you said this . . . (repeating some of what you heard them say) what did you mean? It sounded like you might be (angry, annoyed, frustrated, embarrassed) when you said _____. Is that what you meant to say? I'm just checking to make sure that I really understand."

Acknowledge that you are really listening

    "I don't want to misunderstand what you are saying, so sometimes I'm just asking questions or repeating some of what you say for clarity," you explain. A gentle reminder for you, if you begin to sound like a psychologist or feel fake, your child will pick up on it very quickly, and may very well stop talking because they believe that you are not really listening. It can sound like psychoanalyzing rather than having a Courageous Conversation.

The Gift of Connection

    Provide opportunities to be able to have a Courageous Conversation with your youth, to get them back to the table (dinner table or otherwise). Having those conversations to find out what's really going on in your teen's life and letting them know that you are there for them are essential elements for the growth of connection, and especially for your relationship with your child.

The frame to this is that you cannot have *judgment*, it's really the time for *understanding*. Their life is not your life, it is not your experience, these are not your feelings or your journey. Be there for them and with them. Remember, they are only children once!

Consider taking your teen or young person for a soft drink or a burger, taking the time for individual connection and conversation, particularly if you have more than one child. I know that you are busy, plan the time and make it happen. Your teen is depending on it for their self-esteem and social confidence! They might not say it out loud but think about it for a moment. When was the last time you stopped what you were doing and spent some time with your teen? It has been noted by parents with whom I have spoken that a car ride often is an opening for a Courageous Conversation, as both parties are not necessarily looking at each other and the space provided in the vehicle is close enough and separate enough, without being threatening to the personal space of either the parent or the teen.

Some conversation starters could be any of the following:

What made you smile today?

What was the best part of today?

What was something you saw that made you think?

What was something new that you learned today?

Was there an act of unkindness today that you saw? How did you respond? Could you have made a difference in that situation?

Was there an incident with anyone where you could have stepped in to assist and chose not to? Did you just stand and watch it unfold?

Can you give me an example of kindness that you saw or showed?

Who inspired you today?

Do you think that you inspired anyone today? Tell me more about that.

** *Other questions and conversation starters are available* **

For the download visit:
https:www.elizabethbennettgroup.com

Have Courageous Conversations and *reflective engagement* and practice the elements of the **5 Strategies for Dedicated Listening** to connect with your teen or young person. These strategies will help you to really be curiously engaged in what's happening in their lives and provide tools that can help to support you as a parent. Listen without judgment and wait patiently as you walk alongside, as they try to navigate their pre-teen and teen years. They are hoping like hell that there is a net to catch them when they fall, although too cool to let you know, they really want it to be you who is there for them.

As we deal with ourselves, various situations, circum-stances, and people in our lives daily, we are constantly reacting and responding with the end desire being harmony, safety, caring, and love. However, oftentimes we are merely putting out a fire, solving a problem, or dealing with some sort of crisis. Most of us have coping mechanisms that function significantly well; howev-er, there are those times when we blow a gasket over a trivial event and lose our shit at the first person in our line of sight. Can you relate? No judgment intended, just a moment for all of us to reflect on how we deal, what we say, and how the situation and people are left thinking, feeling, and wondering 'What hap-pened?'

I'd like to enhance a quote from Ross Greene, author of ***Lost and Found: Helping Behaviorally Challenging Students (and, While You're At It, All The Others).*** "Kids will do well if they can." This means we only know what we know at the moment from our family upbringing, our life experiences, and our own way of dealing with things. I would like to augment that quote as follows: "*Parents, kids, and families* will do well if they can." That being said, it becomes the starting point for looking at how we deal with things, our own context and what we believe to be our truths, recognizing our own perspective and the possibilities for new learning. This could also have us look at enhancing what we know which perhaps could use an upgrade. In this next chapter we will do just that. You'll enhance what you know, and perhaps learn a few things that you may not have quite known about your teen.

Chapter 1 Recap

> *"If we have the courage to share, to talk with each other and really be there, the walls begin to crumble; the light starts to break through the cracks, which brightens the path, and we begin to create new relationships with each other."* --Elizabeth Bennett

- Raising a child takes a village: who are you going to include in your village?
- Be vulnerable with your teen and acknowledge them - model it for them.
- Dedicated Listening skills will be handy in all of your encounters - family, friends, co-workers, and in your community.
- 5 Strategies of Dedicated Listening:
  - Understanding vs Judgment
  - Finding Flow
  - Intentional Time
  - Understand First, Speak Second
  - Reflective Engagement
- Don't stress about getting it right - take one strategy at a time and put it into practice so that it becomes a new skill.
- Help your teen to learn these skills so that they will use them in their own relationships.
- Really listen to each other's point of view - it can be the catalyst for conversation.
- These strategies will take time - use them consistently.

Call to Action

➢ Get yourself a journal: write about how things are currently in your relationship with your child(ren). Be honest! No one else has to see what you write. It's a starting point for you.

➢ Pay attention to your own actions when you are in a conversation: Do you dominate? Do you really listen or are you simply thinking of your own response? Record these questions and your observations in your journal.

➢ Pick a time in your day where you can reflect and write in your journal. Consistency is helpful. Make an effort to write every day.

➢ Choose one of the 5 Strategies to work on for a week - focus only on one at a time.

➢ Be vulnerable - take responsibility and model it.

➢ Let go of the judgment of yourself, your child, and the situation.

➢ Lean in like it's the most interesting thing that you've ever done - because it is☺

** Journaling can be an effective way to release your thoughts and feelings which provides you with space for the expansion of learning **

Chapter 2
Getting to Know Your Teen ... Don't Stop at "Fine"

"Just love me the way I am."
"Please take time for me."
"See me." "Hear me."
"Get to know the real me."
"Hold me."
"Love me, no matter what."
"Be there for me when I need you."
"Spend time with me."
"My opinion is important too."
"I'm not always OK."
"I make mistakes too, help me through them."
"The pressure of being perfect for you is really killing me."

These are some of the many answers I received when I asked teens what they wished they could say to their parents. This is what they most want you to know.

Being a teenager isn't easy. The changes going on in the brains of adolescents can make for some pretty intense emotional responses and a greater need for attachment with peers, and at times, dealing with these emotions can feel like living in a pressure cooker. The feeling that you are operating in that environment can lead to frustration, resentment, mental health concerns, and disillusionment about the world. The agony of despair, not knowing if you are loved or important enough at home, while balancing the norms of daily life at school, can be overwhelming.

"Do I have friends? Do they like me? What do people think? What am I supposed to do as a career? Should I take a year off from attending college to get myself together and travel the world? How do I handle this all alone? How will my folks react? How can I talk to them about this, they won't understand?"

As rebellious or as quiet and unassuming as kids can be, therein lies a message; this is a profound display of communication which should be recognized and discussed with your teen, it's your teen's behavior. This is a perfect opportunity to ask engaging and reflective questions to understand the paradox of behavior. Oftentimes their behavior can be displayed as quiet and unassuming, and yet at the same time your teen is paralysed with anxiety, or they can be displaying outward dysfunction in the form of aggressiveness towards you and others which can identify as an underlying sense of fear.

Thought Provoking

Many parents will say that their child doesn't act like this at home, or we never see this type of behavior. It can be noted that at times children and teens hold their shit together at school and feel that their safe place is at home, where they can feel free to let go of their anger and frustration. On the other hand, many teens respond in the opposite way where, according to them, their safe place is at school. Their comfort level, trust, and feeling of safety is displayed at school with a teacher or coach, and many are afraid to go home and let their family know what is going on with them. Sad but true, it occurs more frequently than we believe. What your teen most wants you to know is that they are human, they make mistakes, and they want you to be there for them, not as a critic or a cheerleader; rather, they would like you to be there to support, guide, love, and accept them just the way they are, not as you want them to be.

You see, they can't be you or your dreams, they can only be them, wholeheartedly themselves.

The sad reality is, some young people don't feel like anyone really listens to them or respects them for having thoughts and ideas; in some cases, ideas that can definitely make a difference in the world. Some of our most important entrepreneurs, authors, singers, songwriters, inventors, are young people who thought outside the box and brought those ideas to fruition.

Often, young people get caught up in what their parents' hopes and dreams were and hoping that their kid can achieve success or achieve their parents' failed or unmet, unsuccessful dreams.

What teens most want you to know is that they admire you for your accomplishments, your struggles, your trials and tribulations, and that they want to see you in action, not hiding your disappointment, fear, frustration, or failure.

> *"Children have never been very good at listening to their elders, but they have never failed to imitate them."* James Baldwin

If your child doesn't have the opportunity to see how to respond in a reasonable and responsible fashion as modeled by you, how will they know how to do it for themselves? Being their support system is precisely what your child needs and wants. What 'new world' will your child help to create?

What Your Teen Struggles to Tell You

Your child could potentially be alone. You may not even know if your child has true friends or a girlfriend or boyfriend, same sex or otherwise. All this time they are trying to find their own identity, trying to make it work. They look like they're independent, and they think that they are independent, and no matter what they are looking for you to be there to support them. However, most times, it's still at arms-length. They don't want anyone to know that they still need you. What would their friends say?

Social Isolation

Today's society has us surrounded by social media, phones, videos, Snapchat, Facebook, TikTok; you name it, we have it. However, it is increasing our collective social isolation. It's probably most noticeable with our teens. They often walk with their heads down, their faces in their phones, listening devices shoved in their ears so they can listen to music to drown out the world. They think that those friends that they attach with on Instagram or Twitter, Snapchat or TikTok are friends for life and they're looking for connection, validation, and acceptance. Unfortunately, too many of these social media platforms provide a false sense of security, building an insecure sense of self-esteem, confidence, and reliance on the truth of "online friends." All too many young people are so connected to that false reality that they don't have a real understanding that the majority of their online world are fake friends who show only the marvelous and miraculous rather than the reality of their lives. The influx of social media becomes a place to hide, and an easy place to get acknowledgement from people who they don't even know. Teens are so desperate for someone to like them. When they don't get enough "likes" or enough approval it makes them feel defeated, not wanted, not loved, not accepted. These unhealthy relationships can leave devastating consequences in their wake and often with lasting hurt, feelings of unworthiness, despair, anxiety, depression, suicidal ideation, and even the completion of life. Teens won't tell you when they are struggling. They need to be encouraged to lift their heads occasionally, to look up for just a moment, so they see that connection is right there in front of them, with their friends and family. We are becoming more like our teens when we believe that we can't be without our phones. We also need to lift our heads and reconnect with each other.

What's in it For Them in Movies and Music

The beginning of social impacts:
> What does your teen watch on TV, movies?
> What music do they listen to?
> What video games do they play?
> What books do they read?
> What types of activities are they involved with?

What do they **see and say** on their cell phones, Instagram, Discord, texts, and what do they watch on YouTube, TikTok or any other media platform? Many of the movies that children are exposed to on TV, Netflix, and other viewing locations, often demonstrate an unrealistic view of the world. Although the news illustrates and cites the atrocities that occur, there can be a shift in focus to movies of great creative quality or story time adventures. However, your young person may be more interested in more of the guts, war, crime, killing, and power. This can, from time-to-time, spill over into your child's daily life as demonstrated when being more aggressive in play, in their attitude and behavior, as well as with their language. The types of music or movies might also warrant a conversation regarding the violence, sadness, and despair that tends to ramp up within your child's emotional backpack. I'm not for one minute saying that this happens to every young person or teen, however, it is something to be aware of. It can guide your conversations and help you get to the heart of why these types of shows are so intriguing to them. Watch a movie or two with them, again being curiously engaged about their interest in this type of movie, without judgment. Leave room in the conversation for their opinion and answers, not just yours. "Is it the fast-paced action? The gore? What do you find the most interesting about this movie?" Have a conversation about it. Another way to enhance your understanding of your teen and the deepening of your relationship.

What Were You Thinking?

Your teen does or says something that doesn't quite fit your expectation of them and you say, likely in the heat of anger, "What's going on in that brain of yours? That wasn't the smartest idea!"

Let's take a look at this word cloud image of the brain to see what's really going on.

COMPREHENSION GAMES
MOODS HORMONES LOSS SLEEP
VOICE UNCERTAINTY
ENTHUSIASM **FEAR** AGGRESSIVE
JOY RESISTANCE CONFIDENT BALANCE EATING
PROBLEM THINKING REJECTION HARM LOATHING
FRIENDS PRESSURE UNEASINESS DEFIANT DESPAIR
CURIOSITY LANGUAGE MEMORY SEPARATION SIBLINGS OPPORTUNITIES
UNWORTHY DEPRESSION CONFUSION HAPPY
DIVORCE MOVIES SORROW
RESOURCEFUL WORTH **SELF** FAIL AWKWARD CONTROL
INHIBITION APATHY LAZY SOLVING
APPREHENSION PAIN
UNSURE QUIET LOVE LONELY OBSTINATE INDIFFERENT
REMORSE SCHOOL DRAMA CREATIVE TIMID ALONE WINNING
EMOTIONAL ESTEEM LOSING CAREER VULNERABILITY
ANXIETY MUSIC SEX REBEL
SELF-CONTROL PERFECTION
PARTY RULES CONFIDENCE TALENTS ACHE
PLANNING TEARS BEHAVIOUR HATE
APPROVAL PARENTS INSECURITIES DISAPPOINTMENT
DECISIONS SAD ACCEPTANCE HEART

What distracts your teen? What worries them? What sends them anxiously into a tailspin and out of control? Do you ever wonder why they think that the pressure is too great?

Now, let's match that up with what we know about the developing brain and areas that have not quite caught up with how they act and react. We know that the teen brain is still in the growing and developing stages and that their impulse control centre, or prefrontal cortex, is not fully developed. As a result, the part of the brain that regulates impulse control is not completely attached or wired to their thinking parts of the brain.

That's when you see them do something that you consider to be crazy, like participating in an extreme sport or doing something outlandish. They have a blast, meanwhile you are at your wit's end, afraid of them getting hurt or killed. Or they do something at school, like getting into a fight over something quite menial, and when you ask them "What were you thinking?" their typical answer is, "I don't know" with an innocent look on their face, really being serious in their response. This generally occurs because they often don't know why they did what they did. On the other hand, you are faced with an attitude as big as the day from your teen, equipped with an elaborate story that they have created to justify the incident from their point of view. This leaves you wanting to pull out your hair, questioning how they could make such a choice. Their frontal lobe or forehead area of the brain doesn't truly become fully developed until somewhere between the age of 18-25. Interesting to also point out, research indicates that it is typically completely developed closer to 25-30 years of age.

Let's Talk About 'FINE'

"Hi honey, how was your day?" asks mom.

"Fine," *with a hint of indifference added for good measure,* replies the child.

"What did you do today?" *with an inquisitive tone* parent continues to inquire.

"Nothing much," *moving into apathy,* as the teen approaches the refrigerator for a drink and looks for something to eat in the nearest cupboard.

"What do you mean 'nothing much'? You've been at school for eight hours." Imagine the heightened frustration of the parent as this conversation continues. The heat rises and the tempers begin to flare.

The backpack gets whipped across the floor into the shoe rack, the earbuds go in, the hoody gets pulled up, eyes rolling, face puckering in a mad scowl, and the teen storms out of the kitchen and straddles two stairs at a time to get up to their room. The teen is left frustrated, hurt, and heart-broken, desperate for you to have asked different questions. Meanwhile, still fuming in the kitchen, you're also left heart-broken, not knowing how to connect with your teen. Sound familiar? It's all too frequent a scene, shared with me by many parents. The secret is, if you are continuing to ask the same questions, in all likelihood, the result will be in receiving the same answers. It's not entirely your fault, help is on the way!

As discussed earlier, it's a great time to start your Courageous Conversations perhaps with a shift. Ask to chat with your teen. Start with an acknowledgement of your own reaction and begin to have a conversation to break free of the guilt, resentment, anger, and shame that got mixed within the encounter. Vulnerability is essential. Make a plan to start something new with your child.

"Hey, can we talk? I wanted to tell you that I'm sorry about how things happened today" says you, the parent, and continues, "I just want to know what's happening with you because I care about you and want to know that you're doing okay. It hurts me deeply when I think that we are moving further apart from each other. Do you know what I mean?"

"Yes, I do Mom, sometimes I don't want to discuss school with you because it's not that important to me, and I guess I don't realize that all you are doing is being my mother, worried about me, and thanks for that," says the teenager as they meet you at the dining table or the kitchen counter. An embrace ensues and you both sit together for a while longer talking about how the day had progressed for each of you. It's the reflecting and being vulnerable that helps to make the difference with a connection. Will it be that smooth? Likely not however, it is a pleasant departure from how it had been going with each of you. Give it a try the next time you come to a block in the conversation, see if there is a shift in how you talk with each other. Be responsible for your part in this relationship. It's also modeling for your teen. If they don't see it, how can they learn it?

Time for Inquiry

If there was an issue with your child's behavior, a good way to start would be to ask your teen "Help me understand what's going on that is making you behave in this way?" Sit with the silence, allow your child the time to process both the question and how they are really feeling. Inquire as to where this feeling is in their body, help them to identify their feelings, slowly and carefully. "Tell me more about this" opens your Courageous Conversation even more. Again, it is helpful to sit with the silence and wait for their response. "When you act like this it makes me feel worried, upset, and concerned." Any descriptor that you want to add for yourself helps in order to give your teen a choice of what could possibly be going on for them. Remember, no judgment. This is a practice in patience for you. The scenario could be one where your child feels bullied by their friend in the classroom or at recess. Listen closely to what your child is sharing, verbal and non-verbal clues will be present. As they are sharing with you, ask for further clarification.

"What does it look like in class when your friend looks at you?

"What do you think that 'look' means?"

"Tell me more about what happens with you and your friend."

"What are you making it mean when . . . ?"

Provide your teen with the explanation that not every look has a negative intention, and that sometimes we make up a meaning that doesn't even exist. What if the 'look' does mean something to your child? What could you then say to your child? Inquire into those relationships.

"Today, Sarah is my friend. When Katie is around Sarah won't hang out with me. Katie won't let Sarah play or be anywhere near me," your child describes with sadness in their eyes. Inquiring minds want to know, and that should begin with you.

Speak their Language

Be really honest with your teen and tell them that you don't always understand where they are coming from. Take the time to respect their world, their thoughts, their action, or inaction. They are your children, let them know that you don't have all your shit together, nor do you have all the answers, and you want to work through it with them - together.

What do you remember about school? Did you have lots of friends? Were you picked for activities? Did you enjoy hanging out at recess or lunch, playing or chatting with others and feeling like it was the best time of your life?

Not so much for so many kids.

Many of the questions asked above are equally as frustrating for your child to comprehend and deal with as well. Parents, or should I say caring adults, usually have access to more strategies to combat the chatter in their heads; however, young people need support with those fears, the stress of daily life, and the anxiety created by them, feeling like they must be perfect for you or some other significant person in their life.

Yes! Parents, these are your children. It's okay not to recognize them at the moment, while they are yelling and screaming one minute and smiling the next, being silly, participating in some sort of activity that you have signed them up for, or perhaps they are hiding in their hoodie listening to music and ignoring you. You'll see them wearing a variety of hair colors, tattoos, piercings, and clothes that don't quite fit, either the color or the size. Sometimes they are trying to hide something, and sometimes they just don't know how to fit in. This is a time when they are dealing with a plethora of feelings and emotions. They are anxious about what's happening around them, they are afraid that they don't fit in; they are concerned about the things that are working or not working in their daily lives, and they are definitely fearful about what others say. They are worried about home, school, and their future. In some cases, they don't see any part of it working for them. It is also a time when they're curious and are exploring their sexual orientation, body image or other concerns, and sometimes, because they don't have anyone to talk to about it, they just try to hide it and are dealing with it alone. Teens often have an attitude or behavior that is bigger than the day, and yes, they are still yours. Going through these pre-teen and teen years they are really trying to find their community, trying to find out what's exciting and how they fit in with the trends, so they don't feel like they're standing out or standing alone.

Ishmael's Story

Take Ishmael, for example. He would strut into school with this long black leather coat on every day, with black make-up, black nail polish and dressed all in black, including dying his hair black. At the time it was referred to as goth. In conversations with Ishmael he told me, "It keeps me apart from others, because I don't want to deal with anyone. They are just children and besides, I'm smarter than them, anyways." He did have a big attitude and it seemed to serve him well. Some students engaged in the occasional conversation with Ishmael, but most just took a wide berth, looking to hang out with kids that they could relate to, instead of being with him. He shared that he was having issues at home with his parents and their dislike of his dress, values, and attitude. He was quite rebellious and wanted the world to know it. His parents knew it and had no clue what to do or how to deal with him. After several open and honest discussions that I had with Ismael he shared, "I don't want to be trapped in the same world as my parents, both being accountants, of course doing well, but I don't want to turn out like them." He had a very difficult time describing how he really felt about it, other than rage that he displayed in school and with his dress. I asked him if he wanted to discuss his feelings and concerns with his parents, initially he hesitated, then he told me, "I don't care," being the signal for me to move forward. "I'm going to discuss this information that you shared with me and encourage your parents to talk through it with you." Here's where my Courageous Conversation came into play when I met with his parents and discussed various segments of what Ishmael had shared with me. Through the conversation I helped them to see different perspectives and encouraged them to seek additional support through a family counselor. As one might suspect, they were not in agreement with that, and wanted to deal with the situation with their son privately, by themselves. I acknowledged their preference and inquired, "Now that you know more, how would you progress if you still had the same wants and desires for Ismael, that he did not want for himself? The question was not asked in judgment but rather, an acknowledgement that they were good parents. "The counseling would assist you with different skills and ideas for having courageous conversations with your son, allowing him to pursue goals that he felt were important for him."

As the discussion progressed it became evident that they felt embarrassed about an outsider knowing their personal life story. "Please know that as part of my role I do this type of work with many families. I'm here to support your son in school, and to request or provide direction for additional services in order to assist with supporting you as a family." These feelings that the parents had are very common and challenging, and providing an understanding helped to move them forward. However, it is important to note that change requires action. Action requires effort and a shift in perspective, in order to acknowledge and allow space for personal transformation, and that of your teen. Ishmael attempted twice to take his life before his parents made any effort to take action and make a change in how they were thinking and reacting to their son's bizarre behavior and public persona.

Here's the upside: the practical tools provided within these chapters will help to reframe and re-engage your connections with your loved one. Being gentle, kind, and vulnerable with yourself and your teen, are the keys to opening the Courageous Conversations. It's not going to be easy or instantly rectified if your relationship has been on rocky ground.

It will take time. It is a process that requires patience, empathy, and especially heart centered love, and I know that you have all of that within you.

Chapter 2 Recap

- This is a critical time in your teen's life - so much is going on for them and more often than not they don't know how to handle it all themselves. They'll tell you they are 'fine' and likely, you do the same. Are you going to settle for that because things are stressful for you? Take the time to be curiously engaged . . . you might be pleasantly surprised at the results.

Call to Action

BREATHE: Try this ten second breathing exercise:
Breathe in on the count of three saying in your head, "THINK, FEEL"
Breathe out on the count of seven saying "CHOOSE" as you breathe out
- this will help when you need to regroup before you respond to a situation, your emotions are heightened or you need to re-focus

- ➢ Invite your teen to go to a movie with you - the movie is their choice; buy popcorn and a pop, enjoy the experience with them.
- ➢ Write in your journal after you use the ten second breathing exercise within your day. Describe the impact of having a calm mind and whether you responded differently than you normally would.
- ➢ Invite your teen to be part of meal planning and preparation. Set aside some time to make a few preparations at the beginning of the week.

Chapter 3
Parent – School Collaboration

Your child comes home and tells you that the teacher yelled at them or that something else of significance happened at school. You call the school and **demand** to speak with the principal and set up a meeting with your child's teacher and administration. I get that you likely have steam blowing out of your ears based on something that you heard from your child, and you want the situation dealt with immediately. What things do you think are going on in your child's mind? Will your child be fearful of what could happen in the class with the teacher, their peers or with you when you both arrive home? Again, we are talking about how you show up, not only in the meeting, but also with your demeanor with your child. What will it demonstrate to your teen if you get ballistic with the teacher or the principal?

Keep in mind that there are always many sides to the story; your understanding, as shared by your child, the information that the teacher and the principal have gathered after investigation, and then somewhere in all of that, the truth. Going into the meeting with an open mind, listening and understanding the perspectives, helps for you to gather the information, resolve issues and concerns with the teacher, with the focus of working together to help your child to succeed. Further discussion can then happen with you and your child when you arrive home. Diminishing the teacher or the administration in front of your child does nothing to teach your child how to deal with difficult conversations, but rather it exacerbates the situation and no positive results are provided for anyone.

Teachers and School Staff as Allies

Have you ever felt that you didn't have anywhere to turn with regards to your teen?

It's 3:00 a.m. and you're wide awake because you saw something on your kid's phone earlier and didn't ask them about it, or know what to say to inquire.

Although you might have friends and family who either give you too much support and direction on how to do things, which sounds like you don't do anything right, and, of course, don't you know that they really know far better than you? Or they don't provide enough support when you really need it. This would be a good time to try calling the school *(however, not at 3:00 a.m. insert tiny laugh out loud)* and speaking to your child's teacher. The teachers and other staff at the school your child attends are not the enemy; they spend an incredible amount of time with your child, trying to provide them with a foundation for living and thriving in the world. Teachers and administrators can provide you with an understanding of how your child is succeeding as well as areas of growth that all of you can work on together. There are also a diverse number of agencies that are available for schools to contact on your behalf in order to support you and your family.   Here's a scenario that I've noticed has been happening more frequently. A parent has a situation occur at school, and they aren't quite satisfied with the result. Rather than taking some time to reflect and possibly pursuing additional support and understanding of the situation when cooler heads prevail, they go on social media to share their frustrations and seek out solutions for others about their concern, rather than seeking solution-based results in conversation at the school, with the people who have a fuller understanding of the situation. And we wonder why our kids get involved with this type of behavior. Keep in mind that your child is silently watching.

Again, the situation becomes more elevated. Parents are posting, oftentimes with no resolution or clear understanding of the situation that has occurred in the school or community. Now that the information has been shared and it has gone out to the community without clarity, no back story, or any confirmation of resolution. It creates a (fucking) wildfire that keeps raging with all the comments online, when it could have been resolved with listening to each other, really hearing the other voice and perspective, and working toward a common solution for the benefit of the child.

The snowball effect is massive, which then comes back to the school with more 'cleverly crafted' stories that spread amongst families, with the school personnel being bashed, and no possible solution in sight. The school administration cannot comment on the social media posts, and they are left trying to put out a blazing forest fire with a knotted garden hose. More of a rhetorical question, however not far from the truth, who do you suppose is being bullied at this point? Not only by the parent who didn't feel heard or understood, but now by the cast of thousands who provided their point of view and have likely shared it with their own family. Can you see where this is heading? Once it comes back into the school it often has a detrimental effect on the climate and culture of the school and provides a more challenging atmosphere in the classroom.

Unfortunately, in an effort to avoid feelings of shame, guilt, or otherwise, we lose sight of having a conversation to share, work out a plan, and move forward with action to make the plan work. The result is folks get angry, upset, embarrassed, and then it is taken out on others, usually at home first. This could be your own story, but unless you share with someone, talk out the struggle, ask for help, taking a step out of your own discomfort and shame zone, you continue to stay in the dysfunctional cycle. Whether your struggle is financial or otherwise, taking a deep breath, gathering up all your strength and coming to the school to have a Courageous Conversation might really lead to a win for everyone. It doesn't need to be your journey by yourself, and just so you know, you aren't alone. The intention is not to embarrass anyone, or make someone feel guilty, on the contrary, it is to help things work so that families can get on with life without these extra burdens.

As previously mentioned, the years quickly fly by in your child's life, and there may be times of loss, whether it's a family member or a pet, a divorce or separation, a devastating accident or a time of celebration. These would be important features to share in conversation with the teacher. Establishing this type of relationship early in your child's career assists you in knowing what is going on in your child's school life as well as providing that connection with your child between the home and school. Your teen might not really understand or appreciate it outwardly; however, I can bet that there is a comfort in having you know what is going on with them. It has often been shared with me, after an incident, no matter what the consequence or solution might have been, that students have expressed relief in knowing that their parents were made aware of the situation. Certainly, in conversation with parents, they have also acknowledged and have been relieved in knowing the full story about their child. The relationship that you build with your child's teacher and school administration helps to establish open communication which can oftentimes be of assistance for both you and the teacher. It is incredibly valuable to continue that connection with your teen's school, even when they are in jr. high or senior high school. Parents often believe that there isn't the same necessity to engage with the school when their child is older, through junior high and high school. Parents have commented "that the students should be given space and freedom as they grow and develop." The connection that you establish with the high school is vital for your child's mental health, safety, and welfare. So many added pressures and demands can often derail your child's intentions or pull them astray, and that's when your connection and courageous conversations can be the catalyst to keep them going, even through the turmoil.

Child and Family Services Involvement

This is an area that most people don't want to talk about however, based on the increased incidences of domestic violence, abuse, and other challenging scenarios, safety and obligation prevail.

The folks at your child's school are obligated to be in contact with Child and Family Services (CFS) when and if they believe or suspect that your child is in danger. The thought of having your child swooped away by Child and Family Services because there might be an issue in your home is a very real fear for some parents, but rest assured, this is not an action that is taken lightly. I want to calm your fears with respect to this. Oftentimes your child has already shared information with the teacher which prompts the call. Child and Family Services do their own investigation to determine if the situation is safe for the child. They make every effort to help support the family as best as can be done under the circumstances. Other agencies provide counselling support for families as well as individual counselling for the youth or the parent, depending on their expertise and the need for those services. Community resources provide alternative strategies and courses that can be made available upon request. Parents know the inner workings of their home life and the things that might be important however, they don't necessarily know all of the available resources that can help support the family in need or in crisis. Consider connecting with your child's teacher to help support your child on their daily functioning and support you when and if they can.

Relationships Between Students and Educators

Remember in the first chapter when you were running late, and the morning routine became a whirlwind of commands and demands on your child?

How do you suppose that relationship is going for the teacher with your child in class? How do you think that teen think things are going? As mentioned previously, pre-teens and teenagers don't often have the skills and the strategies necessary to be able to manage to keep a lid on what's going on in their life. The answer really is simple, it starts with conversation, a Courageous Conversation. It's helpful to know what is going on in these students' lives so that they can see and know that they are being supported. Kids need to know and believe that somebody cares about them. It's way too easy for them to slip through the cracks. Rita Pierson professional educator and TED Talk presenter says, "Kids won't learn from people they don't like." I have noticed this has become more prevalent and evident in today's classrooms. Children need to know we care before they'll care.

From my experience as an administrator, I can say with certainty that we still have a few teachers in the system who think that the most important thing is the curriculum, and that's why they are there, simply to teach. We are working on shifting that thought, behavior and action for those teachers however, it's still a work in progress! It definitely is part of their job, but somehow they miss the most important elements, the students and their connection with them.

If the students weren't in the classroom or available to engage, the teacher could not teach. But it's more than that - it's about establishing a relationship, communicating with each other, building a trusting, caring environment for both the teacher to teach and the student to learn. The stakes are high!

It is no longer the teacher who is the holder of information. For goodness sakes, anyone can pick up a digital device and have all the information in the world at their fingertips. The focus of teaching in the 21st century is about engagement, cooperation, collaboration, conversation, facilitation, teaching and learning by everyone. Both the student and the teacher are learners and educators.

Have you ever seen the face of a child who is actually teaching you something? Typically these days it's about the use of technology. It is certainly that for me. Kids know so much more than we ever could. And for me, it is so much fun to ask them to show me how to do something with my phone. They beam with excitement, quickly going through the steps. I learn more about my phone, a program, or a technical malfunction, which seems to happen quite frequently with me, and I am very grateful for their sharing. All that to say that we need to make it work, together.

> Children need to know that we care before they'll care.

Parenting from the other side of the desk - *enter mama bear*

Imagine for a moment, a scene in a comic strip where you see one person on one side of a desk with a megaphone, speaking loudly with their voice blaring through the speaker, and the other person on the other side of the desk is pushed back in their chair with their hair blown back by the volume and the intensity of the words being spoken at them; that's how this meeting started and I was the one with my hair blown back.

Mr. and Mrs. King had a concern about their son and his current behavior and their desire to have him supported in his learning at an appropriate grade level. The blast started soon after they both sat down in my office. I welcomed the parents, we shared a few quick interactions, and then all hell broke loose!

They felt that not enough was being done by the school and by the teacher to support their child, and he was bored and frustrated. As the parents spoke about their concerns, sharing the conversations that they'd had with their son, I listened intently, writing down a few key points that I was going to refer to when I responded later in the conversation. The secretary was aware that I was scheduled to have this meeting, so she was able to take messages and inform folks, if they called or stopped by the office, that I would respond to them as soon as possible.

In conflict management and mediation course training that I had participated in earlier in my career, I recalled the voice of the instructor explaining scenarios similar to this one, *"If you continue to yell at me, this meeting is over."* It rang loudly in my head.

In most situations I would have used that phrase however, I felt that these folks hadn't really been listened to, and this was going to be an opportunity that I could give them to work through their concerns. It was also going to give us the time to create a plan and taking further action together in an effort to come to a solution with the main focus of helping to support their child.

Occasionally, I glanced over to my vice principal whom I had invited to this meeting because she also worked with this family. It was also a great teaching and learning opportunity for her. As she was sitting in her chair diagonally across from me I could see her eyes wide open, probably in shock and dismay, that I would allow this type of behavior to continue. Afterwards I explained to her that in other situations I had chosen to shut down the meeting, re-schedule and support families accordingly until such time as alternative arrangements could be made to reconvene. However, in this particular situation, I felt that these folks needed to be heard, understood, and required a safe space to do that. My gut told me that it seemed like the right thing to do, and as it turned out, they became one of our school's best allies in supporting our programs and providing opportunities for families to feel safe to share their own concerns with us.

As the meeting continued, the "megaphone" was replaced with a calm and a highly interactive courageous conversation. You might be saying that they shouldn't have been so aggressive, but keep in mind, this was a "mama and papa bear" team taking care of their cub. I was not remotely interested in inflaming the situation by telling them to leave.

Patience and dedicated listening saved the day.

I explained in a calm and respectful voice the protocol sequence that was in place regarding a request for accelerating a child to another grade, and I let them know that I would have to inquire about fulfilling their request. We talked through several alternative strategies that we could put into place for their child. We also agreed that we would have a conversation with their child to explain the process, obtain his input and feedback, and help to move things forward. The result was successful for the student and the family after the initial plan was implemented, and arrangements were made to fulfill their request for the following school year. As an endnote to this scenario, there were several meetings, phone conversations, and follow-up meetings to ensure the conversations and the collaboration worked for everyone.

Formative School Connections

Anthony's Story

Mrs. Anderson had been a teacher at the school for several years and had watched the comings and goings of many students, helping those that she could with their struggles and successes. There was, from time to time, a student or two with whom she took extra time or created a connection that was extra loving and caring. Although most teachers say they love and care for everyone equally, there are always a few who pull extra hard on your heartstrings.

Anthony was one of those students. She described him as "bright and cheerful as a young student when I first met him when I was teaching Grade 3 and he was in my class. He was full of life and spunky, I must say. He was such a good student and lovely with all of the other students in our class." Time passed as he went onto other grades, Mrs. Anderson would check in with him every now and then. Several years later, Mrs. Anderson had moved up to Grade 7 as a homeroom teacher and again had reacquainted herself with Anthony when he attended her science class.

She had noticed that he was more withdrawn, would sleep in class and barely completed any of his assignments. She often heard from her colleagues that he was in trouble frequently on the playground and in the community. She wondered what it could be that had made him change so dramatically. Doing her due diligence, Mrs. Anderson was going to put Anthony's name forward to their teacher support team meeting so that she could gain some additional insight and acquire a few more strategies to help support Anthony. She wondered to herself, what might have happened to Anthony?

As she was reading through his school records to update her file, she stumbled upon some notes that were written by his previous grade teachers. In Grade 4 the teacher remarked that 'Anthony was a joy to have in class'. In Grade 5 it was reported that Anthony's dad had a terminal illness, and that Anthony was struggling with attention and completing work in class. His focus was on praying for his dad and he disengaged with the other students in his class. Later that year his dad passed, and Anthony took it very hard. His mother became very distant, so Anthony didn't have anyone to help support him through his trauma.

Mrs. Anderson wept as she continued to read Anthony's file. She had known him and yet, at that moment, felt that she had let him down, not knowing about Anthony losing his dad. She had remembered that Anthony's dad had been his son's champion and superhero. She withdrew her scheduled time with the teacher support team and made a point of searching out Anthony herself, to make arrangements with him during a class change to meet her at the end of the day.

He reluctantly agreed and met with Mrs. Anderson that afternoon. She thanked him for taking the time to meet with her and she informed him that he was not in trouble, but rather that she wanted to discuss the information that she had just learned. She apologized to Anthony for not knowing about his dad and asked if there was anything that she could do to help support him now. He sat with tears in his eyes and thanked her for thinking about him. He told her a bit about his mom drinking and not really engaging, but he was taking care of her when he could, as he was still involved with after school activities. His mother hadn't attended any of the parent-teacher meetings in the past year, so she had no idea how Anthony was really doing. By the end of the meeting, Mrs. Anderson and Anthony had made an agreement to touch base with each other at least once or twice a week to make sure that things were going okay for Anthony. Mrs. Anderson also called Anthony's mother to let her know how things were progressing with Anthony in school. As the year advanced Anthony's work and grades had started to increase, and his disposition in school had also improved. Anthony's mother had called a few times to inform Mrs. Anderson that she was doing better and wanted to know how she could help Anthony at home. At Christmas, Mrs. Anderson received a card and a small gift from Anthony that he had secretly placed on her desk tucked under her plan book. She happened to find it after all the students had left for the day as she was getting ready to prepare for the next day's classes. The inscription read "You're the best teacher I could ever have, thanks for caring about me" signed Anthony. She then opened the gift to find a small key chain with the crest of the Montreal Canadiens, and a little note saying that it was he and his dad's favorite hockey team. She smiled and cried at the same time as she attached the keychain to her school lanyard.

At his high school graduation, Anthony stood before the group of graduates, teachers, families, and guests as the school valedictorian. His remarks focused on having supportive people in life to help you along the journey and he personally thanked Mrs. Anderson for being that person for him.

Years later, as Mrs. Anderson was prepping for her next class, her thoughts of the many students who had journeyed along the pathway to their future came to mind, especially Anthony, as she gazed at the key chain that had reminded her of him. A call from the office had interrupted her thought and she rose from her desk to answer the phone. The call from the office secretary excitedly told Mrs. Anderson that there was a special delivery waiting for her and that she should come immediately to the office. Not knowing what the delivery would be, it wasn't her birthday or any other special occasion, she quickly closed her planning book and headed to the office. There at the office stood this very tall, good-looking guy with a full beard and dark hair, donning a Montreal Canadiens Sweater and holding another one straight out in front of him with the number on the back and the name displayed on the top of the sweater. As Mrs. Anderson approached the office, she recognized him instantly, it was Anthony. She was so delighted to see him that she didn't recognize or acknowledge the sweater, she just rushed to give him a hug. This giant guy hugged her back and they stood in that embrace for a few minutes, while the secretary clapped and cheered them on.

Once Mrs. Anderson stepped back, she wiped the tears from her eyes and asked how Anthony was doing and what was he up to these days. He handed her the sweater with his name emblazoned on the back and gave her an envelope which included two tickets to the next home game. He had just been signed by the Montreal Canadiens and wanted to share the good news and invite Mrs. Anderson to his first NHL game.

"I want to thank you for never giving up on me. I couldn't have done this without you. I would be honored if you would attend my first game. You'll have to check with your principal to find out if you can take the time off, the game is in Montreal." He laughed and continued to tell her, "Your plane ticket is in this envelope and the game is on Friday. Actually," he paused and whispered, "I have already checked with your administration and everything is good to go. You just need to pack your bag." Anthony hugged her again and said that he would see her late on Friday night, after the game.

"Safe travels" she said as they hugged again, and he proceeded to leave the building. She wiped the tears from her eyes with a smile on her face as she turned and looked at the school secretary.

"What a wonderful surprise! I've got to hurry to get back to my class before the bell rings," she said as she gazed up at the clock hanging on the far wall of the main office. Mrs. Anderson walked quickly down the hall to her class, just as the bell rang to dismiss the classes.

We all remember from our own experiences, perhaps a teacher or two, a coach, or other person in our lives who was influential in providing direction for us, listening without judgment, providing ideas and strategies rather than a stern voice only telling us what to do. Many schools around the country and around the world are developing programs and encouraging mentors from many walks of life, to connect with at least one young person within their school or community, to do their best to prevent kids of any age from falling through the cracks and having them know that they have a champion. They are folks who might be bankers or lawyers, mechanics, postal workers or any other heart-centered person, or they very well could be teachers who spend their days with your teen helping them with their academics as well as coaching, teaching morals, values, social skills, and how to advance in the world. They create for your teen somewhat of an artificial sense of family, one where each child is valued, where they belong and are acknowledged for their gifts and talents as an individual human being. Although not every story has a happy ending like this one, it shows the impact of connection and perseverance when someone takes the time to really care. We spend many years with students through their growth and development, and it is essential that the connection and relationship are strong in order to help the student succeed. That is the importance of creating relationships with the school and the family.

Even though these exceptional relationships have meaningful and lasting benefits, and your teen might consider that person one of the most important people in their lives, remember, somewhere in your teen's life there is still a void, and it is that connection with YOU!

Chapter 3 Recap

- When situations at school arise, be open minded while advocating for your child, using a balanced approach.
- Listen, gather the facts, discuss options, be part of designing a solution that can work.
- Discuss with your child for understanding.
- Model a proactive and tempered response to illustrate to your teen how to have a mature, adult conversation.

Call to Action

➢ Be proactive - set up a time early in the school year to connect with your child's teacher.

➢ Set one or two goals for your child to achieve in the school year (discuss them with your child as well so that they are involved and ready to work on them).

➢ Share the goals with the teacher.

➢ Celebrate your child with the teacher: if your child is involved with activities that take time in their life, share those with the teacher so that the teacher can check-in about how your child is succeeding with their activities, it will also give the teacher an opportunity to touch base with you about your child's progress in school.

Chapter 4
Parents are People Too

Unpacking our Own Upbringing

We are often so consumed with our day-to-day activities and taking care of the needs of our family, that we forget about our own experiences. Where did I come from and how did I learn to manage in the world around me, you might ask? How well are you coping? How do you suppose your child is coping?

Home Environment

What type of home-life does your child experience? Is your child made to feel safe and secure? By whose standards, yours or theirs? Are there siblings? What type of relationship do they have together? Is it a blended family? These are questions worthy of consideration when looking at the dynamics that can present themselves, and whether your child has the appropriate coping skills to develop relationships within the context of their family dynamic.

Are there particular issues in your home that you think you are keeping to yourself, that your children don't know about, or so you think? Is there fighting, drugs, bigotry, depression, chronic illness, loss of employment, alcoholism, new job, or career that takes you away from home, general disconnection, worry, grief, fear, or shame? All of these have a direct impact on how your child feels, thinks, acts, and manages in the world around them. Don't be fooled, they can see your mood, your demeanor, your highs and lows, and they can sure feel them as well. How well do you think they are navigating through all of this turmoil in their environment?

Mattie's story

Standing around the kitchen island while grabbing a snack, Matthew shared with his dad how his day had gone. He had really enjoyed the dance class that he had participated in during a presentation at school. Matthew explained that the presentation and activity were part of a resiliency program that the school wanted to share with the junior high students. He had never done hip-hop before and the instructor had told him he was really great at it.

"Dance is for fairies and girls. You're not thinking about doing that are you? Join hockey or lacrosse, not dance. Did you hear that honey? Matthew wants to join dance!" his dad mocked.

His mother could see the look on Mattie's face, and she froze in place, not knowing quite how to respond. At that moment Mattie was swallowed up by embarrassment, he didn't want to cry as he knew his father would continue with the sarcastic commentary.

"Jack, let up on Matthew, he was sharing something that sounded like he enjoyed it. Why are you making fun of him?" his mother exclaimed.

"What's the matter with you kid, can't you take a joke? I was only kidding!" his dad said with a smirk on his face.

"I've got homework to do," Mattie mumbled as he walked around the island, picked up his backpack, grabbed a snack from the fridge and headed to his room.

This is the description of the scene that Mattie shared with me. He said his emotions were all over the place.

"I felt like punching my dad in the face. I was incredibly hurt and at the same time I had 'let him down' by not wanting to sign up for football, hockey, or lacrosse. Sports that he liked. I just had a great time in that class and wanted to do more of it. I even liked when we did line-dancing, ballroom dancing, and other stuff in your class, Ms. Bennett. Although I was shy at the beginning, you just made it fun," Mattie said with enthusiasm, "and it was a blast again in this presentation as well."

> **"*Can't you take a joke?*"** . . . **someone's truth or fear is hidden in their sarcasm**

Imagine for a moment that teasing goes on in your home with you and your teen. Sure, for you it's a joke; however, your child may hear the same thing at school, they don't fully know how to deal with it, they feel shut down, no longer wanting to engage for fear of further embarrassment and then without apparent warning, they lash out at someone at school. What was the teasing for? People assume that teasing is just fun, it's harmless and it builds resiliency. On the contrary, it isn't helping to build anything that will make your child strong, it simply reinforces their belief that they aren't a good person, not worthy and certainly not good enough for you or anyone else for that matter. Do you see where I'm going with this?

You might be thinking, "Can't I ever fool around with my kid?" Of course you can, but first you must provide your child with the tools to cope with these quips, jokes, or teasing. We are so busy assuming that everyone is prepared to laugh it off or let it fly off their back, but rather, in their inner being, your child is absorbing whatever comes their way. Think about it for a moment. Do you believe that they are able to deal well with every situation in every moment of their day? Do you notice that some days are easier than others for you, and of course you are also an adult who can handle it, right?

That may not even be true, and you know it, and now it's a time to be honest with yourself. We oftentimes take for granted that children and adults have the capacity to deal with teasing, bullying, violence, and that they know about empathy, vulnerability or even love, and it is often not the case.

These skills, knowledge, and understanding must be shared, modeled and taught. It's important to know about emotions; what they are, how to acknowledge them within ourselves, be able to express them and know that it is okay to do so are valuable skills to have. A famous quote from Dr. Maya Angelou is "Do the best you can until you know better. Then when you know better, do better." Remember, kids don't have the background of knowledge, skills, strategies, or understanding fully developed, they are still in the learning stages.

I'll add here that we are all continually learning and growing, it's a developmental process that we enhance as we experience situations in life. It's not a 'one size fits all' or 'learn it once and you have it down pat' learning. It takes time and understanding of oneself as one negotiates and navigates through emotional highs and lows. Take the time to consider how you deal with your own emotions as a parent. Do you show them outwardly? How does your vulnerability show up for you? Are you truthful and honest with yourself and others about how you truly feel about things? Are you so busy dealing and helping with everyone else's concerns that you don't take time for yourself? Are your feelings hidden so deep to protect yourself from others? Was your upbringing and home a place where you could share your feelings, emotions, and love openly with others? In the case of Mattie's story he was mocked, belittled, and even scorned for sharing what had happened in his day and how he was feeling about participating in his dance activity. Was his home a place where he felt safe to be himself and be loved unconditionally?

The 'Unquotables' Down Memory Lane, or Quotes we Wish we Had Never Heard

Stop crying or I'll give you something to cry about.
Boys don't cry.
Children should be seen and not heard.
Suck it up buttercup.
Money doesn't grow on trees.
Who do you think I am, Rockefeller?
Be a man about it.
Keep your thoughts to yourself.
Don't talk to me like that, I'm your mother/father.
Who do you think you are?
You're not doing that are you?

You may have heard one or any number of these that are memories in your own emotional backpack, and now you have to let these go and begin to feel safe in your own body while actually letting yourself be free to express your own emotions. That's where it starts.

What's the worst that could happen you ask? Being free from the chains and weight of holding on, pretending you are "fine" when you know that you are not.

'Letting go' can increase the uptake of mood-altering chemicals in your body that increase happiness and lead to healing, reduced anxiety and depression, which creates space for new and expanding emotions such as compassion, empathy, and love. It's not an overnight cure, and it takes time to allow for the change in you, to establish a new nurturing relationship with yourself as well as the new relationship you are building with your child.

Each of us would be the best if we knew how, but if no one has ever taken the time to really show us or model these wonderful values, talked to us about them, or showed us what it is really like to be loved, cared for and honored for who we are, it can be difficult to model these attributes for our own children.

This is your chance to change that – you have the opportunity to change your teen's view of you and of themselves.

Thankfully Mattie's mother was supportive and encouraged him to pursue what he wanted, rather than engaging in his father's suggestions. Noting here that his dad's reaction was likely his very own personal fear of what people would think, rather than encouraging Mattie to participate in whatever would make him happy. Matthew did eventually move beyond the hurt of his father's teasing and really excelled in a variety of genres of dance, both at school and with a local dance studio. He later became the principal dancer for The River Dance International Dance Troupe. He currently owns a very successful dance studio with his sister, and he visits schools in and around his province to promote the positive and life changing benefits of dance. As a result of his visits to schools and the sharing of his story of desire, determination and persistence, there have been a noticeably larger group of male students who have participated in his classes, using the movement in power dance to improve their flexibility, speed, endurance, and strength. He also helps them with their ballroom dancing skills so that they can gracefully move and feel the confidence to ask their partner to dance in more formal settings. Although it took a great deal of courage to share his story with me, Mattie felt that it had empowered him to transform his perceptions and to encourage others to pursue their own personal goals and dreams.

Mattie also said, "Had it not been for my mom, I would have been forced into sports that I didn't want to play. She's been there for me the whole way. She allowed me to pursue my dreams and travelled with me from time to time to support my efforts."

This story speaks to putting aside your own aspirations for you child while taking the time to listen and understand your teen's true desires and being their champion. This next story illustrates the opposite response when the challenges of a parent who believes that his way is the only way and doesn't want to shift his thinking to help support his child in a way that would benefit both of them and their family.

Jonathan's story

Mr. Pascale was quietly waiting in the office when I came in from morning supervision. He had agreed to meet with me a day or two after I had both called and emailed to explain a concern I had with his son's behavior.

The embarrassment in this father's eyes and on his face was evident as he entered the room. He couldn't believe that he was in my office, and yet he was yearning for answers to the dilemma that faced him and his family at home. Sitting down across from me, he placed his hat on the seat beside him. He explained that he came from a family where, as he put it, "Children are seen and not heard, where respect is expected because after all I am the father and the man of the house."

I carefully listened and I heard that challenges existed at home with his teenage son, and they needed to fix it, "…because that is not correct or tolerated in our home," he explained. "He has everything that he wants and needs, I don't understand why he is acting this way," said the father.

Jonathan was born in another country. When his family decided to move to Canada, things were very complicated with obtaining approved documents. As a result of the challenges, Jonathan's mother and father left for Canada to set up their home and settle with the government. Jonathan was left with relatives in his mother's native land. Jonathan and his family were reunited after a few months and things seemed to be going well until Jonathan's attitude and behavior started to turn troublesome. It had become evident that Jonathan was struggling. Jonathan had come from a country whose system of education and culture were very different than it was in Canada. Another factor in Jonathan's life was that twins were born into the family and he was now no longer the only child. Demands were placed on Jonathan to keep up with his chores in the house. These situations were described to me as expectations and orders, according to Jonathan.

Unfortunately, Jonathan's behavior and non-compliance increased at home, the more demands were placed on him.

According to his dad, Jonathan refused to take on his chores and began to spend more time in his room than with his family. When Jonathan did come out from his room he barely ever spoke with his mom or dad. He would eat with them in silence and would hurry to get away from the table when meals were complete. His dad indicated that it was very upsetting, especially for Jonathan's mother, to not have any connection with her son.

Jonathan's deviant behavior also increased at school. He began to start fights and challenged people to take him on in a fight if they didn't believe what he was saying to be true. Jonathan also mumbled unnecessary and sometimes made rude comments, just loud enough for the person to hear, when he walked by their desk or around the tables in the room. When I spoke with Jonathan's dad, I offered a few different strategies and ideas to try with Jonathan in an effort for them to create a connection with each other, differently than the one they were currently experiencing together.

> **Create a different connection than
> the one you currently have**

I encouraged dad to consider spending some quality time just with Jonathan.

"How about if you go to a local coffee shop or to a restaurant, to have a meal together or even just a hot chocolate or a coke? It might be helpful to explain to Jonathan some of the circumstances as they exist, and some of the background as to why he had to stay with other relatives, so that he could understand."

As we continued our conversation, I also recommended that he acknowledge Jonathan for the challenges of the move and his bravery in spite of all of the changes with their family. This would likely provide Jonathan with the feeling that you would understand how he was feeling. That way Jonathan would understand the importance of his efforts in contributing to the household to help support the family, rather than through his frustration. Jonathan currently had only been hearing one way of doing things, usually as orders and demands, and one way to respond—with defiance.

"The individual time with you would provide a listening ear, establish a more connected relationship, and definitely provide an opportunity to shift from the current way of doing and saying things." I had suggested to dad that he listen without judgment, to understand his son's frustration and feelings that may not have been shared previously. I explained to dad that according to Jonathan, "My parents don't listen to me and don't understand."

We made a plan for a meeting with Jonathan and his dad, to provide strategies and another perspective on family dynamics. After having met the parents and having had a conversation with Jonathan, we created a separate meeting time during the school day, to meet with Jonathan to provide strategies for engagement as well as the opportunity to understand his own feelings and give him the chance to work through his grief from the trauma that existed. The impact of leaving his own country and family members, moving to a new home, having more responsibilities and dealing with how to cope at school. Neither Jonathan nor his dad were cognizant that these underlying challenges needed to be identified and dealt with, rather than assuming that "he can manage" as said by Jonathan's dad. It was also explained and suggested to dad that perhaps Jonathan felt abandoned in the parent's quest for security and stability while being in another country, without Jonathan being along for the ride with his parents.

I could see that dad was struggling with those suggestions and just really felt that Jonathan should act accordingly when asked to do something, and he should show respect. The father didn't really understand or want to accept that Jonathan might not have the skills, strategies, or understanding yet or keeping in mind that Jonathan was only 13 years old. It was simply dad's way and dad's rules, no need for any of these explanations or additional conversation with Jonathan.

Several days later, again in my office, after a situation occurred with Jonathan and another student, he and I talked about the incident and the impact that it was having, both for the other student involved as well as for Jonathan. I explained that his escalation in behavior was creating quite a challenge for the teacher and the students in his class. Students were beginning to avoid being near him for fear that they would be the next target.

I started by saying, "Jonathan, I want to let you know that it is alright to be mad, angry, frustrated, and any other emotion that presents itself. However, it's not the place to take out your frustration or anger on other students. You are safe to share them here. I recognize from what you have told me, and what your father and I discussed, from the situations that have occurred in your life, that you need to be able to talk about your feelings in order for them not to cloud your judgment, or your choices of action.

In our continued discussion Jonathan told me, "Kids were not being fair, and they were treating me poorly." It had become abundantly clear that because Jonathan didn't understand how to act appropriately or didn't yet know how to deal with his emotions, he generally responded inappropriately at home and at school. At the conclusion of our visit together, Jonathan was rising to leave and I said, "When you go back to class, just concentrate on what you need to do to get your work done, we will talk more later this week."

A student from Jonathan's class had been sitting at one of the chairs in the office near the door, and as Jonathan was leaving my office I overheard him say an offhanded comment, "I'll get to you later," to the student. I followed Jonathan down the hall, called him back to chat with him, and explained what we had just discussed in my office.

"That comment was unnecessary and would likely not be favorable in trying to make friends with students in the class," I said looking directly at him. Jonathan nodded in agreement, as he had done in the office, and proceeded to his class.

Family Dynamics

Family dynamics can be very complicated and each person within the framework of the family needs to have a voice to describe what they are going through, or even to voice their misunderstanding of life as it occurs at the moment. The filters that exist with the dad in the previous story provide him with only a narrow view of what could be happening, from his own personal life experience. At the same time Jonathan has a skewed view and filter as well, in the way he will hear what his dad's demands are rather than understanding what dad really wants: cleaning his room, putting stuff away, helping out as a demand rather than as a cooperative partnership in contribution.

Some of us come from that expectation of "respect your elders" or get beaten or hit for not responding appropriately or being sent to your room to figure it out. When does sending your child away help to solve the problem? Talking about it can be the very answer that is necessary for the resolution. Thankfully, there are always opportunities for courageous conversations, setting a plan, being your word about what you'll say and what you will do, and taking the appropriate action to complete the request and the plan.

Core Beliefs - Do They Help or Hinder Understanding and Conversation?

We are all too often quick to anger and don't take the time to reflect before responding. This would be a time to determine what your own personal core beliefs are behind the strong emotion, and whether this emotion is something that perhaps was inherited and doesn't fit well or work well in your life now. It provides an opportunity to demonstrate leadership, mentoring, and having Courageous Conversations with your child in order to reach the goals within your family. No one said it would be easy. However, it is a far better way to start working together, than the tearing apart of a family because everyone wants to be "right" and won't budge from their "position" to take responsibility for their own personal action or inaction.

| Working through challenges together can be freeing |

We have become a society who points fingers and blames everyone else rather than owning what we have or have not done, said, demonstrated, acted or not acted upon in any situation. I can hear my own parents' comments in my head and laugh (now) as I hear these repeated in the office where I sat with that father. I could bet money on the fact that my father would have eagerly agreed with that dad, 'just do as I tell you' or expect the wrath of non-compliance.

How can a peaceful resolution come for the family if people are not willing to be dedicated in their listening of each other, through good and bad times, understand and learn about other perspectives, and respect each other in the conversation, rather than it being only "ONE" way? What is the worst that could happen if they tried something different?

Yes, change is difficult and it takes time. Working through the challenges together is freeing and people in the situation can learn, grow, feel connection, feel a little vulnerable in the process, but wow! What are the possibilities? The new love, caring, understanding, and connection that could be made through these Courageous Conversations can be dramatic and truly life changing.

F false E evidence A appearing R real

Our mind, our brain, our body and our emotions play tricks on us to keep us safe. Have you noticed that this is true for most of us these days? We are dealing with the uncertainly of life as we know it; balancing our lives, supporting our families and not knowing what will happen in a few hours, days, weeks or by the end of this year. You may be an office worker whose company has had to lay you off, a small business owner who can't keep their shop open, a large plant employee, a health care worker, a teacher, physician, nurse or a parent who is now working from home, juggling family and trying to focus, or an executive who has been let go after dedicating a career to supporting their company. How will it all unfold? How will you manage? When will this chaos come to an end? How can you maintain some semblance of normalcy in your family? How can you pay the bills and feed your family? These are all legitimate questions, concerns, and anxiety producing challenges that are present.

Are these or any other factors affecting you? Fear, anxiety, depression or worse?

Juggling Too Many Swords

How do you juggle your own adult feelings and concerns while trying to address your child's feelings? I get it, there's a lot that you are worried about, with your family and the outside world; however, it's really important to consider your inner world first, before trying to solve everyone else's concerns or problems. Is your internal anxiety exploding or imploding while you are trying to juggle a million swords, including your family needs and especially all your kids' needs?

Let's look at healing your own past first. This creates a pathway to freedom and happiness for you so that anything that you need to change can be done with gratitude for the learning, grace for the ability to work through it with bravery and resilience, and with love for yourself and your family. Understanding yourself and how you respond and react is a great place to start. This is also a place to recognize that this is your past and it cannot be changed. However, what are you going to do with the hurt and the learnings from your past? How will you deal with them as you move forward in your life?

I know for me as a child, I was a 'pleaser' for my parents because I didn't want to create a situation where they would have an excuse to fight. Mixed with alcohol and a violent temper, my father could manage to create a mountain of trouble from an ant hill, usually over nothing. As a result, I knew that if I had most of the supper prepared, potatoes peeled, kettle already boiled and tea made, dishes away and table set, with the intention to create a calm environment, it would just be a matter of waiting to see which one of my father's characters would walk through the door and how the evening time would proceed. If my father had had a bad day and didn't agree with something that had happened in his workplace, he didn't have the nerve to say anything to his boss or co-workers. He would reach for a glass from the cupboard, the bottle of rye would appear, filling the glass and consuming several glasses of his beverage of choice throughout the monologue, while my mother and I who would sit quietly and reap the unsavory words and feelings of the anger and frustration of my father's rant.

Those times have long passed, and with them the faded scars of those long-ago memories. I no longer respond in that 'pleaser mentality' of my childhood. It has taken a long time to understand why my father was like that and why my mother was a victim of his violence, whether physical or emotional. What I discovered was the generational trauma that was inflicted upon him, growing up in a large family during the depression, struggling for food, working long days in hard, backbreaking work, had shaped my father's attitudes and responses. My mother had a similar background with her parents. Along with the trauma of these events, their modeling was that of a strict, no-nonsense expectation of respectful behavior, physical redirection with a belt or the back of a hand and statements including, children should be seen and not heard" or "don't speak unless you are spoken to." They didn't know any other way, and to them it was the right way to raise a child. My mother was kinder and gentler; however, she still went along with what she thought was expected of her from the people around her.

Many years of participating in professional development, several sessions of hypnotherapy and then becoming certified in that mode of therapy and reading many research articles about brain development and neuroscience, provided me with a better understanding that these trials and tribulations were my father's and my mother's experiences. Although I had been part of them, both good and bad, I could also change how I responded and create a new pathway of thought and action for myself, instead of being at the mercy of those old memories and life.

My persistence, determination, and passionate heart-centred focus based on resiliency, humor, and love has helped me to come through it so that I can guide others on their journey to transform themselves and their relationships.

We often emulate or at least model what we experienced with our parents, whether conscious or not. If they were warm, loving, and caring we want to express those feelings and emotions with our loved ones. If our parents or grandparents were disapproving or absent, violent or otherwise, we want to make our family life better than what we experienced, and we intentionally catch ourselves when we find ourselves falling into old, modeled patterns. We have those patterns in our memory, but we do not have to be stuck living our parents' lives.

Give yourself permission to forgive your parents for whatever you experienced. They did the best they could with what they knew at the time and the skills that they had – after all, if they could have done it differently, wouldn't they have? Let it be about the lessons you have learned and the person that you have become. Let it go and forgive yourself for taking it all so personally. You have succeeded this far, with them or without them. Your parents have been a gift either way and one that you can now share with your family with how you show up for them. Now is the time to imagine what you want it to look like for yourself and your family. It's never too late!

Here's an opportunity to free yourself of your shame, guilt, resentment, judgment, fear, anger and perhaps even jealousy. You can continue to say, "it's in the past, just leave it alone," like my mother says, and you can certainly do that;

however, keep in mind that when you least expect it, your past issues or concerns creep in and show up, create chaos and confusion, all the while you don't understand why. The other choice could be to reflect on the past, take the time to deal with the issues and concerns, loosening the grip they have on you and provide yourself with space for new and exciting adventures and opportunities. Seek out supports, it's not the time to do this on your own. Give up the 'lone wolf' attitude and get yourself out there to learn and grow with others.

It's a sign of strength, not weakness, unlike the myths and rumors out there. Remember, you are not the only one who has ever experienced hardship or trauma--forgive yourself for how you have related or created what you imagine that isn't working and move forward. Only you can do that for yourself. You and your family will be all the better for it!

As your anxiety decreases and you begin to feel settled within yourself, with a newfound sense of calm and peace, it gives you fresh eyes and a heart-centered focus on how to support and guide your teen through their journey from where they are now. As you do the work to plow through and reflect on your past traumas, you will have a greater capacity to use the 5 Strategies for Dedicated Listening to authentically understand and walk alongside your teen.

Chapter 4 Recap

- As a parent, each of your children, perhaps your partner, your job, worries about how everyone is and how they might cope in the day may have your head spinning, and on top of that, there is a project due date looming overhead. Isn't it amazing that we cope each day with this and so much more? When all of those thoughts are swirling around and emotions get stirred up as well, the best doesn't always flow from our brains to our mouths, often leading us to say words that may be hurtful and really unintentional; however, they have just fallen from our lips onto the ears and hearts of our loved ones.

> *"Children have never been very good at listening to their elders, but they have never failed to imitate them."* James Baldwin

- How you respond is critical to how your teen will engage.
- What we don't say is often more powerful than our words. The message that your teen is telling you with their verbal cues and body language is critical. Be watchful!
- Is there only one way to creating a solution to a problem?
- Understanding different perspectives helps to create different solutions at the same time as valuing everyone's opinion.
- Peaceful solutions help to create calm.
- Will feelings of frustration overpower your ability to encourage and strengthen your bond with your teen?

- What's getting in your way?
- How can you help clear the path for yourself and your teen?

Call to Action

➢ Write a letter to one of your parents - describe what it was like for you growing up and what you learned about them and about yourself (mail it, write it in your journal - just for you, or even burn the letter after you write it). It's a magnificent way to release whatever thoughts and feelings that may be trapped in your body.

➢ Apologize to your teen for something you may have said or done, that after reflection you know wasn't the best choice of words.

➢ Write in your journal your experiences with the actions that you have taken.

Chapter 5
Navigating Family Change & Conflict

The Power of Mindset & Resilience

What exactly is Resilience? It can be best described as the ability of a person to either bounce back, rebound or withstand the effects of a situation, and be able to push through and move forward in their lives despite the impact of those situations. I call it bouncability.

When a person gets pushed down mentally, emotionally, physically, socially, financially, and/or spiritually they get up, dust themselves off, wipe the blood, sweat, and tears from their faces, put one foot in front of the other and they get going, again and again and again. The power of bouncability expands as we endure tragic circumstances.

Recently there was a family who came in to see me to tell me that their child was very ill from the effects of chemotherapy. Their teen had stage 4 cancer of the bone and they were asking for our support through prayers. Although devastated by the terrible and heartbreaking situation, they mustered up the courage to find their way to share their story while staying focused on their other children at the same time. Theirs was a message of hope and the desire to ask for community support to help them find strength to endure this terrible circumstance.

We also enhance our resiliency throughout our daily lives, whether it's raising a family, particularly through the teen years, dealing with stress through work, losing a family member including a pet, a client, sales, shut down, stress at home or perhaps dealing with aging parents. While navigating through hardships with relationships and friends or even old situations that creep into our minds, the ability to bounce forward, makes us stronger and more powerful in our effort to move on and rise up.

A friend of mine, Suzanne, called me with regards to her eldest teen and issues that she had been having with him in his school and not knowing where else to turn. She was asking for guidance and support and wondering what to do about his schooling.

"Should my child be in a program?"

"Should he be home schooled?"

"Are there other options that could be considered and pursued?"

She felt that she didn't know how exactly to navigate through the system. As we talked I could tell that she was exasperated, trying her best to keep herself together while she shared with me the many episodes with her son. As we continued the conversation she shared with me,

"I believe that my son is somewhere on the spectrum and all that I want for him is to go to school, do well and be able to graduate."

She felt that the school that her son was currently attending was not supporting her and they just kept calling her to pick him up when he was having an outburst or not dealing particularly well with class expectations. She had been in meeting after meeting at the school, visited her physician to get support, and ended up with medication for both her and her son. She laughed as she explained,

"My medication was to keep me 'up' while I dealt with things, and his medication was to keep him 'down' in order to help him deal with the rapid decline in his ability to stay focused and engaged." After a lengthy time of listening to everything that she had done, places she had gone for support, she just needed and wanted my listening ear to help her vent, reassess what she had been doing, and look for additional avenues to pursue.

Here was this mom trying to cope with the daily struggles of not really knowing what could happen in a moment, an hour, or a day with regards to her child, still advocating for her child. Although challenging, as she mentioned, her main focus was to keep going to support her child and find the best resources for his continued success. This high-powered executive was brought to her knees with the devastating news that her son was ready to take his own life. Her ability to stay the course, find the resources and ask for help was all in the saving grace of her ability to continue to bounce forward.

Bouncability helps us to keep our head up, focus on taking action and keep ourselves moving forward. Now, to have this skill develop, it's going to be important to help teach through conversation and modeling with your child. You cannot save them from every fall, loss or issue that arises in school, on the playground, in their activities, or in the community. Every time you swoop in and scoop them up from the hurt or hardship, it is one less time they learn to fall down and get up on their own. Your teen needs to understand that they can reflect, learn and grow, and eventually work with their newfound skills that assist them in adapting to the situation, responding appropriately and moving on.

We need to encourage our young people and teens to celebrate the hardships as well as the successes. Celebrating the hardships is what really empowers teens and gives them strength, determination, and persistence to push through challenging situations. Sure, it is going to be hard and you can be there alongside when and if you can; however, it is critical that you don't "save" them every time. Many kids these days have the tendency to quit rather than really learning how to accomplish something that might be hard at the beginning. The secret to whether they try again or give up is their mindset. When hardship is celebrated, and they are encouraged to stay the course, this assists them in developing a growth mindset (the more I challenge myself, the better I become), rather than a fixed mindset (if it's hard, you don't have what it takes). Similar to when they first learned to ride their bike. If they fell off once did they take the bike home and never ride it again or did they, *with encouragement,* pick themselves up from the ground, get back on and continue to try until they accomplished the feat of riding? The same can be said for anything new that they will learn as a young person or even as an adult.

We live in a 'throw away' society which sometimes includes throwing away our hopes and dreams because it is difficult or challenging. A hockey player, a parent, a rock star, dentist, skateboarder, lawyer, skilled trades person, nurse, teacher, an Olympic athlete or any other profession or career, do not become an overnight sensation. They work long and hard, through many trials and tribulations, and usually come out the other side successfully equipped to proceed into the world.

You are here now, desiring to learn and grow. Take a breath, exhale and smile acknowledging your accomplishments as a parent, a partner, a friend, perhaps a sibling and definitely someone's child. Be with that, take it in and be reminded of everything that got you here, that is worthy of celebration. It's important to take the time to have each member of your family do the same. We are often too busy to take the time for acknowledgement of each other or being grateful, and it gets forgotten in our daily lives which tends to diminish our worth and self-esteem. The lack of acknowledgement often leads to poor self-image as well.

In a program that I was recently leading we suggested two activities that families could participate in together. The first activity was to gather and discuss the word 'accomplishment'. When that conversation was complete each family member was given a blank piece of paper. They were asked to write a list of all of their accomplishments and when they had completed their list they were instructed to share the list with their family. As the lists were being read aloud, the other members of the family could contribute to each other's list. At the end of the meeting the lists would be posted in a central location for everyone to see and to add to when they accomplished something, or they saw their other family members accomplish something.

The second activity instructed the parents to find a medium sized jar, label it "with gratitude" and have a conversation with their family about what gratitude meant to them. The 'action part' was that they were each asked to cut up paper into small strips and leave a pen or pencil beside the jar with these little pieces of paper. Preferably placing the papers and jar in a central location - the kitchen. Every day for a month, each family member was given the task of writing something that they were grateful for on the small slip of paper and placing it in the jar. At the end of the month each family was asked to gather together, empty the jar and read through all the notes of gratitude and share them with each other. When we met with the families at the end of that challenge, there was an exhilaration of love that was palpable. I encourage you to try these activities with your family.

YOU'VE GOT THIS and so will they, with your help and loving support.

Big Family Changes

Underlying Dynamics - Where Do We Go From Here?

The scenario that you read earlier about Jonathan and his father is a perfect example of the complexity of a person. Many aspects had not clearly been identified and perhaps have not ever been dealt with, and yet the father was convinced his response was one that would solve or rectify the situation in his mind and in his son's behavior.

Let's take this apart and identify some underlying areas that could require some support for this student and perhaps for his parents as well:

- Jonathan's parents were preparing to leave his homeland and start a life in a new country.

- There could be room for a family conversation detailing some of the steps that would need to take place. It became clear to me through discussion with dad that this conversation didn't happen with any depth, based on the information provided by the father and his description of the details. In all likelihood the son was just told about their leaving, and that was the end of that story.
- The parents were leaving their homeland to organize their life in their new country, their son was left with relatives. Perhaps there were some abandonment concerns with Jonathan that at some point would need to be addressed.
- His parents needed to settle their emigration requirements and it was best to leave him, in their minds; however, that was never addressed with their son, and I am not certain it was even taken into consideration. Jonathan was with family, 'it would be fine', as stated by the dad.
- If you look at it from the parent perspective, how easy would it be for you to leave one of your children behind? Sit with that for a moment. Now, here is Jonathan at only 13, look through his eyes and imagine what he was possibly going through.
- This child now arrives in this new country meeting his parents after being separated from them.
- He must attend a new school, meet new people, and follow rules within the school and community that are not familiar to him.

Now, we can all make assumptions and we can presume that he should just be able to fit in, build resiliency and cope. However, we are dealing with a real live person who might not yet have the skills and strategies to manage this all on his own.

We all could assume, and mistakenly so, that "he'll be fine" "he'll make friends" without recognizing that this young person has also come from another country with different rules, norms, and certainly a different culture with strict expectations. Now he is in a place where the school environment provides more freedom, flexibility, and vastly different expectations than that of his original homeland. With little guidance and understanding, Jonathan's ability to cope with this newfound freedom was also more than this young man knew what to do with in an appropriate fashion. The experience was fun at first, yet daunting at the same time, and trying to fit in made it even more challenging. As a result, his schoolwork and his behavior both declined rapidly, and even with re-direction and support, it quickly went off the rails.

> It takes a village to raise a family

The suggestions that were given to the father were an effort to encourage him to have a Courageous Conversation with his son. Had this occurred, there may have been an opportunity to support the son through the upheaval, reduce the possibility of his continued defiant behavior, and have a greater understanding of his son's feelings. As previously mentioned, these courageous conversations require a follow-up and check-ins so that everyone is given a chance to express their feelings and is being heard throughout the circumstance. Ex: moving, divorce, separation, or other major family life change.

Reframing Difficult Behaviours

Let's look at this first approach to understanding how you are perhaps responding to your child and what you believe they are capable or incapable of doing:

When you think your child WON'T	Where's Your Mindset? (as a parent)	When you think your child Can't YET
Perhaps your child has been a bit willful and defiant. ***"Won't you do anything right?"*** *says the parent . . .*	What's your view of your child?	Are you curious? Looking to understand the situations with the intention of looking to find a solution to support your teen?
How are you helping with their willfulness or defiance? Are you butting heads because you both want to do it your way? Power Struggle?	What's your child thinking? Feeling?	Are there too many things that are heavy for your child? Too much stress (home and school?) Do you see any deficits or areas of concern about your teen?
He's just plain lazy! She's just looking for attention! How rude - oh, that's just their way!	How do you respond to their needs?	What's perhaps holding them back? What might be getting in their way? How can I help them with it or through it?
I'll take away your favorite thing if you don't do "this". I'll buy you your favorite thing when you get "this" done.	Do you know what their needs are?	Find the thing that is holding them back and do your best to remove the barrier so that they can proceed (take action, complete the task etc.)
Feelings of frustration, guilt and shame, resentment, powerless, resignation. "Why Bother?"	What experience do you think that your teen is gaining from your interactions?	With this encouragement your teen is likely to feel supported and strengthened in their desire to achieve/do more

If you find yourself exhibiting maladaptive responses as a parent, you can reflect upon your behaviors and see the challenging moments that you have experienced and have displayed. You can then reflect and readjust to make every effort not to act in that way in the future, particularly when responding to your teen and their behavior. Acknowledging any errors in your own judgment and taking responsibility for your actions is critically important in that situation.

You can go through the same process with your teen by being a detective of sorts, through curious engagement to find areas in their life that are possibly stressful. Taking on this role and having courageous conversations, helping them identify their feelings, acknowledging them and inquiring as to how to work through their challenges, will give an opening to assist in reducing their stressors. Asking them about what they need and supporting them in meeting that need will help them to feel heard and understood. If there are deficits or areas that require strengthening, this would be a great time to help teach them, modeling and explaining the impact of making these changes.

Inquiries as your guide to being curiously engaged could include:

"What's going on for you when I ask you to put your clothes away or clean your room? You seem to get mad about it. I don't want it to be a fight every time. Do you think that you could you explain it to me so that I can understand and perhaps help you through whatever's going on?"

"You mentioned that the school counselor was in your class presenting about how to apply for high school courses. I bet it feels like a lot of pressure. Talking about it sometimes helps to create a clearer path in order to make a decision. What are your thoughts about what you might like to choose? What are you thinking that you would like to do?

What Does Kindness Look Like?

Now it's possible that you may not be familiar with exactly how to teach your child to be kind, because perhaps you didn't have anyone in your life demonstrate how to be kind. What does it really look like, feel like and how do we really put kindness into action?

We all just assume that when you say something like, "For God's sakes Jason, you're in Grade 7 and you are acting like a Grade 1 student." Jason will intuitively understand that you are asking him to behave in a suitable manner, unfortunately he doesn't know what it is he is supposed to do, say or how to act. It's likely because he doesn't even know or have the skills that we assume he should have based on his age. I have been known to say those things as well and then in my reflection and follow-up with the student, I ask if they know what these skills really are, and if not, I begin to demonstrate and teach what they look like so that they have a future reference point and example of what could be possible if a situation arises in the future.

If your teen at home is not seeing or having these appropriate behaviors modeled for them, ones that we consider important and respectful, how do we expect them to have these skills? Some of these skills could very well be lagging, as illustrated in Ross Green's book "The Explosive Child". Kids simply might never have been taught skills like patience, waiting your turn, respect, kindness, and empathy to name just a few, because no one before them had known these characteristics either. "You can't teach what you don't know." Teach kids skills - they won't know if you don't teach them. Acknowledge yourself for the work you have done with your teen and know that they still may have challenges. It will take time.

> *We typically assume 'they would if they could'* Ross Green

The heavy weight we collectively place on young people and teens to be and act in a certain way, and the weight they take on from the worries that creep into their existence, it's no wonder we have kids with high anxiety disorders, maladaptive behavior, and kids who "flip their lids" in class or at home when the situation becomes unbearable. 'Flipped lids' is a term used to describe what the brain does in response to an incident or action. Do you recall the situation at the beginning of the first chapter, remember the stuff that went on in that teen's life, waking up from a sound sleep, the response to their clothing choice, "the most important meal of the day" lecture? All of this is leading to 'the boiling pot' just in that morning prior to getting to school. Look through their eyes, be in their shoes for just a few minutes and see for yourself how difficult it is for a young person or teen to not "lose it"! And for those who are capable of holding it all together at school, they are looking for a safe place to unload. How can they cope if they don't really have the skills and strategies to deal with everyday events?

We need to give our kids permission to explode, flip their lid or do what they need to do which could be crying, getting angry, yelling as examples, so that they can unload the pressure of what is going on for them and within them. We need to be okay with all of it and encourage them to throw it all at us until they get rid of it all. Provide them with a safe place, allow them the time to get rid of the built up emotions from their bodies, let it all just hit the floor. Your teen needs to know that all these emotions are healthy, and it's going to be important to be there to walk through it all with them. It's not the time to send them to their room and have them work it out. What's there to work out? They don't have any idea why they are feeling like they are, it might be a combination of hormones, fear, anxiety, depression, or any other emotion you can imagine.

> **Stay with them, so that they can fall apart with you, so that they can let go and you will be there.**

Bring them nearer to you, rather than sending them away. Although we have heard about 'time outs' they are not always the best remedy. Why send your child away when they really need you now? Perhaps it might be more appropriate for you to excuse yourself for a few minutes so that you can regain your own composure and then join them to re-engage in conversation or listening to what is really going on for them. If you respond with heightened intensity your child will model that, then what do you have? This is where your patience is required instead, sit with the silence, the yelling and screaming, the tantrums. Hold them, draw them close if you can and if they will let you. Let them know that you really love them, hug and hold on, because sometimes words alone aren't enough. Be with them, no matter what. Not between emails and texts etc. just with them! If that means that you must make alternative arrangements because you had something on your agenda "suck it up buttercup" and change it.

YOUR KID NEEDS YOU, RIGHT NOW! When your teen has calmed which, by the way, might take a few hours, it will then be the time to review the situation when they can calmly communicate and acknowledge their feelings. That's when you can model empathy, talk and discuss how to try to handle similar situations in the future. The key ingredient in all of it is for you to be there with them when and if it happens again. Sure it's calm now, we provide strategies and think that it's all good. They know what to do now, because we have said so. But what happens on the playground when someone doesn't share the ball, or gets them out in a game, or says a nasty word, or pushes and shoves in a game of soccer or in the hallway or in class, when some half-assed comment gets thrown their way? Although you can't be there for each moment in their day, your use of kind words and actions, providing them the safe space and knowing that they have someone to share these feelings with, can often assist your child in holding it together until they can be with you.

Is the picture becoming clearer? That's when we need to be there, in their hearts and their minds, to coach, to support, and to have them be part of the conversation, working through the issue, again and again. They are not going to get it the first time, or the sixth time, we simply have assumed it should click in soon. We know instinctively that it must be practiced and supported with encouragement, modeling, listening, and understanding. It takes "action and demonstration" a teaching and learning moment every time. It's who we are! It's imperative for your child or children to know that they are truly loved by you. It's part of the missing link!

How Much to Tell the Kids

Do you remember hearing the phrase "children should be seen and not heard"? I remember when I was growing up important information that was discussed by my parents was not shared with me. Although I could hear my parents argue and fight, sometimes violently, I was never part of the conversation about what was going on. The world back then was veiled in secrecy. It was a time when families kept secrets, they had challenges in their lives and thought that they were the only ones who had these problems and that they were alone to solve them. Besides, no one would understand. Most important of all, you don't share your family concerns with strangers!

The Swinging Pendulum and Other Stories

The pendulum has definitely swung way in the other direction. Children seem to know all too much of the inner workings of issues and concerns of the family and so many other things they are exposed to these days, including the "information of the moment" shared by Facebook, Instagram, Twitter, TikTok, and other social media platforms. With that, what teens see, and what they believe they know, they are all too eager to share whatever intimate information they have heard with whomever will listen, especially with their friends and often with their teachers. Unfortunately, sometimes this knowledge of the misunderstood elements of adult conversations can play havoc with a child's mental health including increasing anxiety, fear, depression, anger, guilt, and resentment. This occurs more often that most people know and it happens because of something that might have been overheard while adults in the home were having a conversation or worse, yelling at each other over issues that the parents hadn't yet figured out for themselves.

Children often don't know the context of the conversations being discussed and they often take what they hear personally and internalize it. Some teens share everything with someone they trust, while others don't want to talk with anyone, especially their parents. Others share the highlight reel and the filtered photos online but are reluctant to share the deeper stuff, while many share their whole life story and more with total strangers online. They very well might be sharing vastly different stories with friends than with their parents.

Chendaya's story

A student came to see me when we were organizing a field trip for her class. She had just delivered the field trip forms to the office.

"Thanks, Chendaya, are you excited about going on this field trip?" I asked as I walked with her down the hallway towards her class.

"I can't go," she said, as she looked away and muttered the words more softly.

"What's going on?" I inquired.

"It's because my parents don't have any money to be able to pay for me," as she looked up at me with tears in her eyes, "we don't have any food at home."

My heart sank instantly, taking a deep breath and trying to compose my inner self, I assured her that she would not miss the fieldtrip as we would figure something out. After Chendaya returned to class I met with our counselor and began to create a preliminary plan to help support this family. We contacted the student's mom to see how we could help. Although appreciative and shocked at the same time, Chendaya's mother assured us that her family was doing quite well, and she wondered how her child could have shared such a story. The mother was also quite concerned about how we would have made that assumption and asked if she could come to the school to have conversation and clear up any misinformation.

As it turned out, I was dealing with another scenario when Chendaya's mother arrived so our Vice Principal invited Chendeya's mom into her office, with the counselor present, mom had also asked that her daughter be allowed to join in the meeting. When I arrived to check in on the meeting, I slipped into the room and stood quietly as I listened. It turned out that Chendaya had overheard a conversation between her parents and had misunderstood information that she had heard.

"I thought that my mom had lost her job and that we didn't have any money or food. I was worried about our family, and so when Ms. Bennett asked me about the field trip, I told her about it."

Chendaya's mom was very grateful that we would have helped her family and she assured us that her family was not in peril. She paid for her daughter's fieldtrip at the office and signed the fieldtrip form, gave her daughter a hug and kiss saying, "Don't worry my child, have fun today and we can talk more at home, I love you." Chendaya's mom headed out of the school on her way back to work.

The following day, Chendaya came through the front door of the school, headed directly to the front desk of the office with several bags of food as a contribution to the food drive.

"My mother and father said thank you and they wanted to help others who needed it." Chendaya said, as she laid the bags by the other food items that had been collected for a local charity.

This illustrates how easily a conversation can be misunderstood and the impact the story has when shared from the innocence of a child's perspective. We know full well that this can even happen to adults when they don't have the complete information of a story. The misinformation becomes bigger than the facts and, mixed with a variety of feelings, can create havoc before the story is sorted out and truths are shared.

There may be times when you are addressing a serious issue behind closed doors, and you do not want to share it with your child or children; that is your prerogative. However, if they are within earshot of your discussion, it is helpful to share with your child enough information about what is happening in the family to help them understand the situation without overburdening them with worry. We know that we have no control over how the message is interpreted by the person with whom we are sharing; however, it is still important to explain as best as possible so that your child or children have a picture of what is really going on. A suggestion is that parents ask their teen to explain in their own words what they had just heard their parent tell them. Then the parent could continue the conversation with further details or confirmation of information shared.

"Use your own words and explain back to me what you have just heard."

"When I explained to you what was going on, how did it make you feel?"

"When I explained this to you, what did you hear? Tell me about that."

"What are you thinking now that you have heard my explanation about what is happening?

> **Look at the impact of a story
> when it's misunderstood**

Facing Adversity Together -
How you respond is critical

Brenda was crushed by the news that she received earlier in her day. Her job was being outsourced and she would not be required any longer at the company where she had worked for many years. As she drove up the driveway to her home, she saw her children playing on the street with some friends. She waved casually in their direction as she picked up the mail from the box at the front entrance to their home. She threw down her purse and computer bag on the bench in the hallway and headed to her room to get changed. How was she going to tell her family about this latest development? How was she going to pay for their activities that she knew were due soon?

Brenda was a relatively new widow who had lost her partner in a skiing accident, coming up to nearly a year since their loss. The kids were old enough to understand her pain and grief as they also had their own to deal with. This was going to be another crushing blow. Brenda contemplated what she would tell her kids about what was going on; however, she wasn't sure how they would articulate how they felt. She would deal with that as it arose. Pulling on her husband's t-shirt and her running shorts, she continued to work through what she was going to say. It would take time for her younger daughter to process however, she was confident that her teenage son would be 'fine' with it. It wouldn't bother him much, she assumed.

Brenda wandered across the street to the park to chat with her kids about what they thought they might do for supper. She told her kids that she was going for a run and that when she returned, they would head home together. As Brenda started her run, her head was spinning with thoughts about how she would explain her situation to her kids, giving them a chance to hang out at the park for a while longer. When they did arrive home, she invited her children to sit with her in the living room and asked that they not turn on the TV until she was finished chatting with them. Jason jumped on his favorite chair, with his legs dangling over the arm, and Jesse snuggled into the corner of the couch that she so rarely got to sit in, because that was mom's normal spot. Brenda had chosen to sit on the footstool that sat between the couch and the armchair so that she could see both of her kids as she spoke with them.

"Listen you guys, I want to start by saying everything will be 'fine' when I tell you about what happened today. The company I work for is changing some of what they are doing, and I was told today that I no longer have a job at that company," Brenda paused briefly, took a breath to calm her inner turmoil, and continued to explain. "Lucky for us we have some savings, so you don't need to worry about not being able to join your activities. It will all work out. We'll be 'fine'." Brenda checked in with both of her kids through her gaze. They both appeared to handle the situation well. No questions yet. "Let's go out for dinner together. Where would you like to go?" their mother said as she rose from the stool and put on her jacket. They made the decision together and off they went to dinner.

Further discussion occurred at dinner and Brenda left it there, changing the subject to focus on the kids and their day. She felt like it had been dealt with and the kids had seemed okay with it all. A few weeks passed and I had to call Brenda because her son had been in a fight during a game at lunchtime. She indicated that she would be at the school within the hour, and when she arrived and sat with me in my office, she told me what had happened with her job.

Michael had been at the office, explaining his part of the story and had not shared their personal information, he just told me and his mom the same story, that "Some kid pushed me when we were playing our game and I pushed him back, he punched me first." Brenda thanked me for telling her about the incident. She and her son were accepting of the suspension and said that she would call me to let me know if there was any additional information that she could provide. Brenda picked up both of her kids and they headed home.

The following day Brenda left me a message, I returned her call nearer the end of the day, and she explained,

"Michael had been frustrated and worried about me, and when another student had pushed him the other student had made some comment about me that Michael took personally, so he hit the kid." Brenda explained that she would spend more time talking with Michael and Jesse, her younger daughter, separately so that she could explain more about her job and help each of them to share their feelings with their mother rather than taking it out on other people. Brenda also knew that there had been lots that had occurred within the year, so she would be more mindful of what to share with her children in the future. She also inquired with me if there were school resources or a therapist in the community whom she could see. She thought it would be a good idea to seek out some family assistance. I gave her the phone number of a few community resources. Brenda's story illustrates that it is important to discuss issues and concerns that will have an impact on the family dynamic and each individual within the family. Brenda also took the time to reflect for herself and have a conversation with each of her children separately, so that she could monitor their responses and behaviors accordingly. She demonstrated as well that seeking additional supports could help to reduce the possibility of anxiety and other concerns that might arise for both of her children, as well as for her. Knowing that assistance was available helped to reduce Brenda's worries as a parent, thankful that she didn't have to do it all alone.

Abuse, Divorce & Diagnoses

When a child has been the victim of abuse, parents are frequently unaware that this can and sometimes occur in their home, with a family member, a close relative or a family friend. This trauma definitely has detrimental effects that the child may or may not be displaying at the moment, and your child may not want to disclose or tell you about this event and however long it had occurred. From stories that have been shared with me, the common one is that the teen has conjured up a story in their head that if they tell you, all hell will break loose. They don't clearly recognize that you would be grateful for knowing, so that supports can be put in place to help.

However, oftentimes the teen is too ashamed or feeling guilty because they believe that if they had done something differently, this would not have happened to them. They feel responsible, and what a heavy burden that is on any child. These were similar feelings to what I had about telling my father that our landlord had abused me. I didn't tell my parents because I was sure it would have made life more miserable for my mother and me amidst my father's already abusive background and alcoholism. I was ashamed, embarrassed, and just so afraid! I never did tell them. I get that it should have been a good thing to tell them, but then I thought I would never be allowed to go anywhere or do anything without them worrying. Do you see how the mind can work and how the committee in my head took over, trying to protect me?

Here are a few things to watch out for. As was suggested in an earlier chapter, your skill in being curiously engaged with your child and asking those difficult questions or acknowledging that you have noticed changes, is the way to start your inquiry. Please be advised that the following examples are illustrations that may show up for your child. These are not meant to be absolutes, simply a few suggestions to use for inquiry. These symptoms may also show up for your child in other scenarios that we discuss within the book.

You may notice that your child has withdrawn from friends or usual activities, so ask them about that. You could say "I've noticed that you haven't been hanging around with _____, what's up?"

You may notice that your child has been displaying changes in behavior: more subdued, not engaging in conversation, they may be more aggressive or withdrawn, displaying defiant behavior, depression or anxiety may be heightened.

Your child's attitude and behavior may result in more frequent absences from school, wanting to hide or not be noticed.

They might demonstrate a reluctance or hesitation to leave school activities because they don't want to go home.

There may be attempts at running away because they want to avoid any contact with their abuser.

They may choose to self-harm, like cutting or burns on their body, or make attempts at suicide.

Another scenario that frequently arises is when a family is going through or perhaps have been through a divorce or a separation, and now the family and your partner are no longer together. Think for a moment how that has impacted your life, it could be a happy time for you or it may have been devastating. Now amplify that feeling for your child. Their understanding is usually incomplete or even skewed, depending on the type of separation and divorce you were going through, and the conversations that were either shared with your child or any bits and pieces they overheard. What courageous conversations have you had with your child about this loss in your family?

Most of the time when tragedy strikes children think it had something to do with them. What are you going to say about that? How are you going to help them understand that sometimes relationships don't work like we think they should? It could be that one or both partners weren't committed or connected in the relationship. Sometimes we hold back what we are really thinking or feeling which disrupts the trust, caring and integrity within the relationship.

Those are the conversations that are important to have with your teen. Show them that you too can be vulnerable, that crying is ok, getting angry or downright mad is also good, as long as it is done in a respectful manner and not at someone. Emphasizing that feelings are acceptable to deal with so that they learn to develop strong, committed relationships, develop trust, have compassion, empathy and love. Discover together that there is more than one way to understand a situation. That's what should be happening.

If your teen is listening to all the conversations that you're having within your home, those fighting, violent, screaming disagreements and disruptions, what effect does that have on them? Don't think for a moment that they don't know what's going on. How can you make it different for them? Yes, you are going through the turmoil and so are they. Unfortunately, they may not have the developed skills, knowledge, and disposition to be able to handle the situation well. Even as adults, we don't do particularly well. How can we then expect our child or children to have all the answers, go to school, act normally, focus, pay attention, work hard, and deal with a life altering scenario at home? Add on challenges that they possibly face at school, learning difficulties, homework, exams, their future, college or university, holding down a part time job, bullying, not fitting in, not a great home life, perhaps not eating or sleeping well, and all the while they think that they are supposed to show up as the perfect child. What pressure!

If your teen now spends time between two households, they will most likely see and hear things from each home that are conflicting and hard for them to fully understand and handle. There's a chance that it is very challenging for your child on every level. Keep in mind they have their own relationship with your ex-partner, separate from you. The loss, grief, sadness. and despair will be separate from yours. Oftentimes children are not taken into account or considered with regards to breakups in adult relationships. They are simply told that it wasn't about them. Think about that for a moment, how would you understand that if someone said that to you, even as an adult? Granted, not every divorce or separation is an amicable one, and as such it is important to do your best as a parent to have a conversation with your child, to have them explain to you how they are feeling so that you can understand and support them. In situations where there is less communication with the former partner, it is vitally important that the child's needs are taken into consideration with both parents. Your child's safety and well-being are at stake.

Depending on your teen's age, they may not fully understand the impact on their own emotions or how to deal with this loss. It is a trauma which, left unattended, can often lead to dysfunctional behaviors. It is not all a bad news story, leaving your relationship may have been a saving grace and could have saved your life and that of your child. I'm just bringing to light the experiences and information that I have had the privilege to know and want to share with you so that you have knowledge, tools, and strategies for a stronger and more powerful relationship with yourself and with your child or children.

DJ's Story

The backstory is that the parents of this child had separated; the mom took the younger sibling to live with her while dad had custody of DJ, the older brother. An absolute heart-breaking story that was shared with me shortly after I was introduced to this child. A feisty little character, DJ arrives in my office, rapidly and convincingly explaining about a situation that had just happened on the playground.

"There was this pushing and then the other guy punched and then something else happened, and he did this, and they stood and shouted," explained DJ in a heightened state of excitement and speed as he told the story.

I'm sure you are getting the picture. I bet by now you have noticed that DJ has not spoken once about his own actions or his personal involvement in the incident. It gets better, he never does tell his part. My regular visits with DJ also provided me with information that led me to believe and understand that the faster he spoke, the more involved and deeper in trouble he was regarding the incident. He always wanted to tell his story first, before any of the other students or teachers reported their point of view of the happenings. A few times in his flurry to get to the office first to report, he would run into people or knock stuff out of their arms in his excitement of wanting to share his story, not realizing or caring about the impact upon others left in his wake.

Visits and conversations with DJ became much more frequent as he was having difficulty focusing in class. His attention span in class was extremely short, with louder than normal responses to group questions by the teacher. He would shout out answers, even when not asked, he would get up close and personal with other students, either to get and gather their information for an assignment or by reporting on them because they were doing something that he didn't approve of. He would get really upset if he felt that he hadn't been invited to participate in a group within the class and would then disrupt others.

His biggest attraction was to be a smooth talker with the secretary; come into the office, often uninvited, and then begin to share stories. As time went on, we came to find out that hardly any of DJ's stories were ever true, as confirmed by his dad. In the early stages, DJ's visits to the office were both because of incidents involving him, as well as suggestions by his teachers that he needed 'time out' from the class. He always knew the right things to say and would happily engage in adult conversations, assuring any of us that he had it under control and would do his best, either back in the class or at lunchtime during activities. DJ's behavior in and out of the classroom escalated and his times became much more frequent at the office, usually with me, the Vice Principal or with the counselor, prompting the need for additional strategies. His dad had been contacted several times so that he was aware of DJ's behavior and antics, and then the dad was invited in to discuss additional strategies to help DJ get back on track.

When dad arrived at school on one occasion, he admitted that he had been having a few challenges at home with DJ; however, he was surprised about the number of times that DJ had been causing such a fuss at school. Several of the situations were discussed, and the dad shared with us the version of the stories that DJ had been telling him at home, obviously noting that they were dramatically different than what had actually been reported at school. More incidences occurred at school, some of which were just redirected either by the teacher or by the supervisor on duty at lunch. More one-on-one conversations were had with DJ by various school staff, all with the intention of trying to provide a teachable moment and re-directing him to do more appropriate steps in his learning.

None of his actions were enough for a time away from school, as we were using progressive discipline; however, dad had been informed that should outbursts, distractions, and inappropriate behaviors continue we would start with in-school suspensions to help keep DJ focused on his work and remove the distractions, which seemed to increase his behaviors. Dad also agreed to the progressive steps and asked about any other strategies that he could use at home to help support the school. It was also suggested that the dad make an appointment with his family physician for DJ, to have the doctor rule out medical conditions.

What did come forth from the doctor visit, several weeks later, was a diagnosis of ADHD (attention deficit hyperactivity disorder) and ODD (oppositional defiance disorder), subtle or otherwise called mild, yet clearly observable. The purpose of mentioning these disorders is not to judge or label the student, rather the diagnosis provided information and strategies that would be put into place within the classroom during transition times and free time at lunch. This was to assist in creating a safe place for all students in the class.

By chunking smaller bits of instructions and tasks, providing simple step-by-step directions and support for DJ's learning, it was also an effort to acknowledge DJ's positive behaviors while providing strategies for diminishing disruptive and dysfunctional behaviors. That was great for us to implement in class, and dad also said that the physician recommended a prescription that DJ could take if his dad agreed. DJ's dad came back to discuss the doctor's findings and asked about the medication. I'm not a proponent of putting kids on drugs; however, from time to time the drugs help to reduce the distractions and assist students in focusing and regulating their behavior. In this case it turned out to be a benefit for this student.

The example I use to describe the 'focus concern' looks like this: imagine for a moment that you have an enormous wall full of televisions with each TV showing a different channel or station, and your child is asked to focus only on one TV in the center of the wall. Can you just imagine how difficult it would be for that teen to focus attentively to only one TV? The medication will often reduce or blur out the other TVs, reduce the outbursts, help to regain focus, and reduce the immediate response of the dysfunction that is just ready and waiting to jump out at any time. Without medication, this child is left with the outcome of the outbursts, usually not in their favor, and consequences quickly following with little or no remorse for their actions because they really couldn't control themselves in the first place. That was exactly what was happening with DJ.

The other Courageous Conversation that was had with dad was focused more directly on the trauma that he as a parent, as well as his child, had experienced with the separation from his wife, DJ's mother. Although dad seemed eager to listen and often agreed during our meetings, he didn't follow through either with seeking his own supports or the resources that were provided for him through and by the school. He felt that he could handle the situation and they would be 'fine' on their own.

The impact of that situation, as well as the decision to re-direct DJ, was significant for him as he continued to struggle with engaging appropriately with his peers and was craving attention from any adult who would listen. The effects of not thinking about the fallout or impact on DJ when the dad was regularly portrayed as a buddy, rather than setting more structured boundaries for his child, and not supporting the recommendations from the physician or from the school only increased the struggles that DJ tried so hard to fight.

Although as educators we are not medical doctors or psychologists, we do our best to provide strategies and suggest resources to assist families in dealing with the underlying impact of devastating trauma. In that particular case, we were attempting to mitigate the dysfunctional behavior that had been identified as the outward manifestation of the deeper, more complex challenge of the separation and abandonment. The strategies and resources that we then suggested were to deal with those particular concerns.

Trauma and Mental Health

It is also important to note that domestic trauma as well as trauma inflicted upon children and their families from various circumstances, as in escaping from war-torn countries, refugee camps, seeing death and destruction firsthand and so much more, have created a mental health crisis of incredible magnitude. We are all part of dealing with it as these children enter our schools and families begin to engage in school and community activities. We make every effort to work with these children and their families in the schools as they integrate into this new learning and living environment. Often, schools have specialized programs to help support the students with language, learning and understanding a new culture. We also help parents engage with community agencies to support their needs in their new homes and in their community.

What's Possible

These two scenarios are just a snapshot of the complexity of situations that exist within our students' and families' lives, in our communities, and in our schools.

This transition doesn't necessarily only exist with families moving from other countries. This could also be a family moving from one area of the city to another. The loss of friends, comfort, and security might be the trauma faced by the child and their family. This could also be a family who has now had the devastation of separation, divorce or death. We need to be cognizant of the impact of transition and how to support effectively. Even though these traumas are personal, it's always important to be attentive to your child's needs, so when your teen requires assistance as a result of displaying inappropriate behaviors, not engaging in activities or in class for example, more resources can be suggested and provided to the family so that they have the understanding of wrap-around service from the school, the family and the community.

Chapter 5 Recap

- Is there only "one" way to creating a solution to a problem?
- Understanding different perspectives helps to create different solutions at the same time as valuing everyone's opinion.
- Peaceful solutions help to create calm.
- Be careful not to diminish your child's feelings. Although unintentional, it can happen without you really knowing.
- Refrain from using words such as: "*don't be silly, you don't have to feel that way*" or "*it's easy*", "*forget about it*". These thoughts don't leave your child's mind very easily.
- Keep in mind that 'your way' of thinking and responding is only 'one' way. Allow space for those "BIG" emotions that your child is dealing with.
- Be open to the possibility of seeking help for yourself and/or your child so that you can have assistance with dealing with major challenges. We aren't meant to have all the answers. It is not a weakness, rather it's freeing, as you allow your courageous self to ask for help.

Call to Action

- ➤ Have a conversation with your teen about something that is occurring in your life or in theirs or a current event. Use the skills of paraphrasing while you are engaging in conversation and listening. Have them recount what you have said to them in their own words. Practice this skill with them so that they have the opportunity to use it as well.

Chapter 6
Talking Through Teen Struggles

Social Media, Cyber Safety & Cell Phones

Vulnerability isn't So Bad

Taking off your mask and helping your teen remove theirs. Being vulnerable, being courageous in thought, word, and action is what is needed to truly understand each other. Our youth can't see the opportunities that are right there in front of them. That's where your Courageous Conversations and connection with them needs to be focused. The obsession and possible addiction to social media and video games is certainly on the rise, and as the need to be connected to this addiction seems harmless, it creates even more powerful companions; a skewed sense of reality, false sense of security, and social isolation. All of these can come with dire consequences.

Who is Your Child Interacting With?

Today's children really have some questionable role models when it comes to social media. There are 'perfect faces' and 'beautiful' bodies that are almost impossible to actually have unless you aren't eating anything of any substance or binging and purging in an effort to match what the teens imagine to be real body shapes. Aren't filters and photoshop great? There are young folks who have thousands of followers and our teens are following these 'stars' who do crazy shit, put it on TikTok or Instagram and then share it with "youth groupies". YouTube sensations who don't tell the whole story of their life, only the stunningly beautiful rendition that they are hoping is believed.

And then there are those predators who lure innocent young folks into believing that they are meeting other young people of a similar age. They are being seduced and, in some cases, invited to take inappropriate pictures and sending them to God knows who on the internet, never to be retrieved again. The unfortunate stories that have been shared with me have escalated in the past few years. Unfortunately, most of the parents I have had to share these events with had little or no knowledge of these incidents. This is not a judgement. Most teens know what they are doing and don't share that part of themselves with their parents. And they are most likely going to continue these types of actions or behaviors unless parents become more involved with what their children are watching, doing, and saying online.

We can no longer turn a blind eye or say, "We are giving them a little freedom and we don't want to invade their space" . . . oh YES you do! In speaking with our police service and personally attending professional development courses focused on internet safety, cyberbullying, and trafficking, the recommendations are to have a conversation with your child. Take the time to search through their apps, their chats and anything else that you see that might have hidden layers on their devices. Tell them that you will check their cellular device from time to time and that it gets parked in your room at night.

This leads me into this next story about a young woman, Sophia, who was seduced by a young man on Facebook several years ago, telling her that he loved her and wanted to become more intimate. Sexting increased, texting sexual advances, promises of love and devotion, and then she was finally asked to send intimate pictures of herself to him. These intimate pictures included half naked or even fully naked shots of her body that she had sent him. At that point, when the story was shared with me the thought *'What were you thinking?'* remained in my head as I listened to the story. Fully appreciating that this young woman was desperate for love and attention.

"He told me he loved me. I was going to find it any way I could," as she explained it to me.

Further investigation continued with the support of the local police service and the young man was eventually apprehended. His parents were informed of the situation and arrangements were made to redirect the student to another school, remove possession of his cell phone, and he was regularly monitored by the police technology unit. The young woman was encouraged by the police that she should tell her parents and, with support from our school administration, we met with Sophia's parents to provide counseling supports for their child and strategies for the appropriate use of her cell phone.

Although it was a traumatic experience for the families as well as with the two students involved, the saddest part is that sexting and sexual inappropriateness online happens far more frequently that we know about. The teens that I have spoken with usually know some of what they are doing. However, often it is acted out in secret so that their parents are unaware of the type of connections and behavior that is conducted over the internet. Unfortunately, the teen rarely understands the complexity of impact this type of behavior includes. All too often parents are left trying to scramble to get their child's pictures shut down from the varying social media outlets, the teen is left devastated, embarrassed, and constantly concerned about the responses elicited by their parents and their friends at school.

Social Impact

More and more teens and in-betweens are spending waking and sleeping time scrolling, chatting, and gaming throughout the night and we wonder why they can't get up in the morning or stay awake during the day. Social media is really an oxymoron, as it should be called 'social isolation'. Too much time is being spent on having their head down looking at their device and not enough time with their chin up, interacting with those live human beings around them who love them and care for them.

You might have noticed that your teen doesn't seem to bring friends home or doesn't engage in their preferred activities with the same passion they once had. Ex: social activities with friends, playing their favorite instrument, dance, athletics or other sorts of activities. These warning signs can be cause for alarm bells ringing in your body. Checking in with your child is an important element in creating a sacred bond with you and not the false sense of security that video games or social media pretends to provide. Here's another place where you can have a Courageous Conversation with your teen to create powerful relationships that are sustainable, not fleeting, like the ones on TikTok or Instagram. Provide them with tools to engage in these conversations with you and really listen to what they are saying.

A short time ago I was at brunch with my partner when I noticed this couple at the table diagonally across from us. The gentleman had a cell phone in his hand and was so engaged with it that he didn't appear to have any conversation with the woman he was with. She sat quietly across from him. It was like both of them were by themselves. I was watching their interaction, or should I say lack thereof, and felt really sorry for both of them. What are we becoming that we can't interact with each other without the use of a cell phone?

Thankfully there are still groups of people who choose to take on the playful challenge of placing their device in the center of the table, with the agreement from the group that whoever grabs their device first pays the bill for the group. What a marvelous idea!

We know that as adults we aren't much better at it! It would be advantageous to set some boundaries around the use of cell phones while eating together, playing a game or watching television or a movie together. This provides an opportunity to practice and demonstrate a little self-control and at the same time helps to reduce the incessant scrolling and text checking, and redirects the collective focus to conversation etc. It's important to teach your children about moderation and the appropriate time and place to use their device. It takes a bit of time to discuss while engaging in understanding everyone's perspective, using the 5 Strategies of Dedicated Listening. Making a plan together will be far better than the authoritarian approach, this is also where a courageous conversation would take place. It also encourages a new habit of appropriate use and responsible digital citizenship.

Schools have created rules around cell phone use and have established policies in order for their students to focus on their schoolwork and assignments instead of texting and sexting with each other.

There was a time not so long ago when I would take and accept cell phones at the office from teachers who had frequently reminded their students about being digitally responsible. At any given time I would have 2 or 3 cell phones in my office and, while doing work of my own, these devices would whirr, hum, buzz or play some sort of theme song while vibrating on my desk. The funniest thing about it was that it assisted me in tracking down other students who were also using their phones inappropriately during class, as their face would light up or a message was clearly posted on the screen of the phones that were parked on my desk. I would promptly walk to those classes and request to speak with the student whose messages had just been relayed to the phone. I would have a brief conversation with the student, retrieve their phone, and remind them that they could pick up their cellular device at the end of the day. Annoying as it was for them, most students certainly got the hint and made better choices through the year. Others, not so much.

From time to time parents were contacted and invited to pick up their child's cell phone at the office because of repeated offenses. On several occasions parents asked that their child's cell phone be kept at the school for a few days, and that they would have conversation with their child about using their phone responsibly or losing it for a period of time. Although it created anger with some students at being caught, more of them got the message and tried their best to use their devices wisely. Unfortunately, a few parents had to be reminded to call the office and leave a message for their child with the office staff instead of texting their child in the middle of the day. Did they forget that their children were at school all day? Other parents needed to be reminded that the school office needed to know when kids were sick so that they could support the students, rather than having parents arriving to the school seeking to take their sick child home without the office knowing anything about it. It became very disconcerting for the office staff.

Eventually a survey was distributed to parents, students, educational assistants, and teaching staff inquiring as to the use of cell phones in classes, as well as the management of cell phone use at home, in order for the school and home to work closer together. Parents who responded to the survey had a variety of answers regarding their own personal management and agreed that cell phone use in school should be limited.

Student responses certainly gave us a better indication of how cell phones were being used or misused in classes. The students also provided honest answers about their own personal safety and the misuse that could possibly harm them, either at school or in their community. Many students felt that cyberbullying was increasing and they didn't feel safe about that happening to them or their friends. Their opinions were quite surprising and, although a small group wanted to revolt and insisted that their rights were being violated, we listened intently and provided them with the results of the survey so that they could understand the bigger picture and the impact that their choices were having on others, particularly during teaching and learning time. These survey results led to the creation of a cell phone policy in our school, that basically restricted the use of phones during school hours, to the relief of the majority of teachers and students.

It was a challenge for the first while, but it sorted itself out a short time later. We had further discussion with teachers who had been using their technology in classes with their students conducting polls, surveys, current events, online quizzes, and learning games. They inquired as to whether that type of activity would still be available as a teaching tool. Although we understood their requests and the importance of a variety of teaching and learning methods, we suggested that the use of alternative methods through laptops or Chromebooks within the classes would be more appropriate for the time being. It was also suggested that activity on these devices was much easier to monitor by the teacher in the class.

We agreed to review the situation and respond accordingly later in the school year. Our focus was clearly on the reduction of incidences with cell phone usage. This included the rigorous supervision by teachers in classes as well as the ongoing support of parents. The monitoring of cell phone use outside of school was, and still is, a challenge and unfortunately issues and concerns often came back into the school in the form of bullying, name calling, isolation, aggression during games, nasty words, and actions in the halls and in classes. Those events lead to time-consuming discussions, investigations, and in extreme cases suspensions from school.

Many students felt that they didn't have anyone to talk to when these situations got out of hand, and they became anxious and hyper stressed. They often felt trapped within their stories that were being shared, including gossip, rumors, 'hate' texts, perceptions in some cases that were not even understandable. Although feelings of guilt, shame, and embarrassment were expressed it was ever so helpful to have had the opportunity to meet with the parents, for them to understand the circumstance, and be the advocate for their child in those particular situations.

Social impact doesn't seem to be part of the skill set of some youth. They believe what they hear from their so-called friends and other social media connections as gospel. Their understanding of situations has often been so far off the mark and yet their perceptions take over, rather than being able to listen or understand reason and rational thinking. Prior to conducting our surveys, many parents inquired as to how to control what goes on with cell phone use at home. The following are some of the suggestions that were shared through the parent survey that we conducted, as well as recommendations that we also shared with parents when they asked for support.

1. Continue to monitor your teen's use of their cell phone.
2. Be intentional with your conversation with your teen about who they follow on their media platforms.
3. Have regular conversations with your teen about what they say online and the types of interactions that should be avoided.
4. Set clear and reasonable expectations regarding usage, which should include daytime and nighttime use.
5. Decide where the cell phone sleeps at night. You might recall that we had the conversation about Dedicated Listening, so be sure that you ask what your teen thinks, listen for their responses, continue to talk about being reasonable and responsible.
6. Include a conversation about boundaries. What will cell phone use look like within your family? Will there be set times when everyone will have time free from usage?

You will get some pushback regarding reducing cell phone usage; however, if you are able to model what you want to set in place, there may be a reduction in negative attitude and behavior.

Here are a few conversation starters that you can begin with when you are inquiring about how you child interacts on their cellular device:

"So . . . give me an idea of what goes on when you're on your phone."

"Help me to understand what is happening in your social media world."

"What types of things do you typically search for?"

"What types of things do you talk about with your friends?"

"I noticed that you responded in your text like you were mad . . . how do you think your friend will respond?"

"I wonder what it must have been like for your friend when they received that text . . . tell me more about that. What were you meaning to say? Do you think it sounded like that?"

"How do you suppose they were feeling when you said such and such?"

"Imagine if that was you who received that text. How would you have responded?"

This last example doesn't always work because sometimes the response is "It wouldn't matter," or "I'd be OK." This is evidence of your teen not acknowledging or knowing how to express their own feelings. Ask about why it would be OK or why they wouldn't acknowledge their feelings about that certain issue or concern.

This is the deep dive into discovering what is going on in your teen's head and heart and beginning to readjust your thinking and help them through those feelings. Dedicated listening really kicks in here, when you are actively engaged, asking questions for clarification and trying to understand all the nuances of your teen's story. Draw out the details and have them explain them to you so that you clearly understand. Assumptions here could be catastrophic. Be really curious, listen without judgment and say it to them. Repeat back to them some of what they are saying so that they have the opportunity to hear it differently. Assure them that you are not trying to be a therapist, but rather, wanting to know more about them. This helps them to agree or shift their thinking, their feeling, their fear or their explanation of the story with real emotion. Acknowledge the emotion or lack of it as they explain more of their story.

Building the connection starts to happen here. The trust, honesty, and vulnerability hopefully reduce the stress and anxiety that they have been carrying for so long. The heaviness that teens carry often makes them go deeper into the rabbit hole of the internet as they seek for reassurance, escape, connection, although superficial and artificial, it beats how they feel about their own reality. However, unfortunately it is not the cure for their mixed emotions, depression, uncertainty, and the pressure they all too often carry on their own.

Think about a time when you were speaking with a colleague or a friend, telling them about an issue or concern that you were having, and they were listening and interjecting their solutions or comparing it to something that had been going on with them. Did you feel listened to, or did you feel derailed and undervalued for your vulnerability and sharing of information with this person? That's typically how teens feel, always being redirected, diminished for their thoughts and feelings, 'don't be silly' comes to mind again from conversations that I have been part of when a teen and their parents have been in a meeting with me.

It's time to acknowledge teen's feelings, look through their eyes, be in their shoes and try to imagine what it really must be like for them in this situation. Ask if your opinion and suggestions are wanted or needed, keep inquiring, listening, and walking alongside. The power in these strategies is beyond magical when you really take the time to engage in them with your teen.

These are ongoing strategies for you to consider and to use, keeping in mind that nothing changes with participating in this type of Courageous Conversation sporadically. It is an ongoing development and enhancement of strategies, including being vulnerable, making dedicated time, and valuing your child as a growing and thriving real human being who has a unique mind of their own. Someone who really wants it to be you who is there with them for the long haul, through their discoveries, their setbacks and their victories and success. The responsibility is massive, are you up for the challenge?

Friend Drama

I had a situation with two young teens, Jessica and Katie, who were complaining about each other and the things they were finding out about 'what was being said behind their backs'. This is a typical statement from students when they are angry with their friends. I spoke with each of the students individually to hear their perspective of the trouble that was brewing.

Katie described it like this,

"I was mad at Jessica because I had heard from Nadia that Jessica thought I was getting to be too stuck up and wasn't nice to her (Jessica) anymore. We used to be best friends; I don't understand why Jessica is saying that about me. I told Olivia that I needed to take a break from Jessica. That's all I said."

Not knowing all the details of the spat her friends were having, Olivia then happened to share with Jessica what Katie had said. Unfortunately, Olivia enhanced the story and added a few elements of her own, which made Jessica livid. Jessica then reported,

"Olivia told me that Katie didn't want to be my friend ever again, and she was sick and tired of me always hanging all over her and sticking to her like glue. Now I'm mad and it hurts my feelings because she's supposed to be my best friend. And how come I heard it from Olivia? Now Katie is talking behind my back."

Doesn't this remind you of the game 'telephone'? Where people stood or sat in a circle and the leader whispered a statement in the ear of the person sitting beside them, then that person whispered the statement they heard to the next person, and the sharing continued until the message came back to the leader in the circle, who shared the received message with the group. The message that was created by the original sender is then shared with the group. Comparing the final response to the original message is quite remarkable as they are seldom the same. This illustrates how people interpret what is said to them and how they share what they have heard, using their own words and ideas of the message they received.

That's what happened in this story, with a little embellishment from Ms. Olivia. Keeping in mind that the fastest way to discuss an issue is on social media, Jessica promptly started texting, and texting, and texting hurtful and spiteful statements to her friend, Katie. And as we all know, texting does not usually stay between two people, a larger group of friends naturally had to weigh-in on the drama. The friendship naturally disintegrated and both friends were devastated. Anger, upset, embarrassment, and a ton of other emotions were mixed within the situation, as you can well imagine, including continued gossip from the others who chimed in on the situation.

The school counselor and I assisted with breaking through the drama, collecting individual accounts of the information from all of the girls in the group, and working with both students to resolve the situation. Several months had passed and things seemed to have improved between these two 'friends', when I received a call from Katie's mother, requesting a meeting.

Katie's mom and dad arrived and informed me that they were wanting me to keep the two girls apart, and that the texting and emails had to stop. I inquired as to whether the parents had been checking their daughter's texts and emails and they both indicated that they trusted their daughter and wanted to provide her with space, considering that she was mature for her age. They didn't feel that checking her cell phone was necessary.

We then met with Katie, who indicated that she was feeling attacked online and that things had gone from bad to worse. I told Katie that I was confused, knowing that I had seen her and Jessica from time to time engaging with each other, laughing and walking to classes together.

I encouraged the parents to contact the police to report their concern, as much of this situation had occurred outside of school time. We had a School Resource Officer attached to our school, so I contacted her for additional suggestions and support for the families if they so requested. The SRO also was invited to the classes to discuss the situation and encourage all the students to follow the school policy and be good digital citizens, which meant being responsible for how they conducted themselves online as well as in person.

Coincidentally, Jessica's mom called me the next day and had a similar request, to keep the girls apart. I indicated that it would be a bit of a challenge considering they were both in the same class, and I assured both families that we would discretely share the information with the teachers and make appropriate arrangements within the classes, which included rearranging seating assignments, as is done from time to time by teachers for different projects. The teachers were also asked to not have the girls in the same groups for activities or projects.

Within days of making those arrangements, Katie's mom called again and requested another meeting. This time she came in to tell me,

"I had in fact checked Katie's cell phone and discovered that Katie had been the one who had also been sending inappropriate messages to Jessica." There was silence, you could see the look of shame and embarrassment on Katie's mom's face.

"Thank you for the suggestion and support. It was very difficult, and my heart sank as I read through Katie's posts. I appreciate all your support and guidance; it has been very helpful. I have spoken to Katie, and I know there will be more to discuss when we are home together," Katie's mom said as she rose from her chair in my office.

She informed me as well that both mothers had also reconnected, as they had also been long-time friends. They made amends and proceeded to make connections for the families to meet and start a new relationship. The good news was that the girls, with the help of their families and the new skills developed through working with the school counselor, as well as their own individual family counselor, provided them with a stronger bond of friendship within each family and with each other for the remainder of the year. The not-so-great news was that this situation in its entirety was over a two-year period.

The moral of the story, emphasized as well by our School Resource Officer, was that parents are legally responsible for the contents and information that is shared through cell phones. It is the parents who pay for the phone and who the phone is technically registered to when signing the official documents. Therefore, it is important to have a conversation with your teens about appropriate and responsible digital citizenship. In other words, choose to use it wisely or choose the consequence. It's also important for you to share the ground rules with your child, for example,

131

"If there are issues, I will need to see your phone. It's not about trust, it's about resolution." It might also be possible to prevent things from escalating by inquiring into your child's relationships.

Seeking Acceptance

If there is any type of trauma within the home, your child could perhaps experience difficulty and not quite know how to deal with it in the most socially acceptable way. Often, they will:

- attempt to get others to like them or hang out with them in an effort to deflect from the uncertainty of emotions rumbling inside of them.
- crave love and understanding.
- want help but are not quite capable of asking for it, so they take it out on someone, just to get the hurt, fear, shame or guilt away from them.
- be jealous of someone who is having fun, someone else who always has friends around them or someone who they think looks weaker than them, so they lash out at another person, finally being powerful over someone else.

Generally, they do not really know or comprehend the extent of the impact of their emotional blowout. This can be a place where you begin to recognize the dysfunctional behavior.

Some teens withdraw from activities and no longer engage with their friends or they get overly involved with activities, taking care of others to push the hurt away as far as possible, faking like everything is 'fine'. Here's where you will want to inquire as to why you haven't seen your teen's friends.

"I haven't seen Carly in a while. Why aren't people coming over anymore? Did you have a fallout or an argument with one of them? Let's talk about it. Perhaps I can help you look at your options. I'm not going to tell you what to do, I just want to hear about how it is affecting you. I have noticed that you have seemed a little different lately, much sadder looking. How can I help?"

Don't expect that they will respond with open arms and tell you everything, especially if they know how you have typically reacted in the past or that you always have an answer. Give yourself the time to wait and work through it first, if they don't take you up on your offer right away. Your teen will most likely be surprised that you have actually noticed what's been going on with them!

What are THEY Going to Say About It?

Teenagers often struggle and don't really know how to engage with their peers. They just see someone else having fun and they aren't having any fun, or they want to be included and they don't know how to ask or don't want to be rejected, so they don't bother asking to play.

Other things that occur as an example, playing soccer at lunch. Your teen may have missed kicking the ball to pass or to stop a ball as it scores on their team and someone yells out "You suck, you can't even kick the ball!" This devastating statement in public, in front of their friends, creates a desire for the ground to swallow them up so they will no longer be humiliated. I can hear you say, "What's the big deal? Get on with playing!" It is a major deal, being embarrassed in front of your peers. *"Will they pass the ball to me again? Will I be left out? How do I get better if no one passes me the ball? How can I get to play on the team? Will they pick me to play or will I get picked last, like usual?"* Your teen could potentially be able to ignore that comment because they already know that they play well. It was just a fluke in missing the ball and they don't really care what the other kids think. Or they really hide it well and say they are 'fine' if anyone asks. It could be the case that they don't have the best soccer skills, they are on the field and no one passes to them; frustration and disappointment occur and they feel left out. These are just a few examples of what happens on the field.

Another example is that your child is aggressive when playing and may not care or recognize that they constantly hurting others by barreling through everyone while their effort and focus are solely on scoring. This is an opportunity to ask questions to inquire as to how they see their playing engagement with others. Questions that you could ask:

"Are you aware of others on your team or do you hog the ball in order to score? Do you pass the ball and play as a team member? Tell me more about how you play when you play soccer at lunch. Who do you play with? Give me an example for me to understand how you play."

These are all great questions and conversation starters to weave into your discussion.

"Who is on your team? Is your team usually the winning team? Are the teams fair or do you have most of the best players on your team? Tell me more about what happens. Who picks the teams? How are the teams decided each day? Are you the boss of your team? Do you help other players by passing to them to let them try scoring or do you only pass to the other good players?" I usually make an effort to watch the soccer games at lunch; however, there are times when I've been called away to support someone and I don't get to see every game.

When students arrive in my office due to some incident after lunchtime soccer, I often ask these questions as well, to know and learn about the dynamics of the situation. The opinions of the players are varied; however, the common thread lies in the approach to the game. When I have spoken to students about their playing, I have frequently reminded them that their game is not 'game 7 of the World Cup'. I encourage them to take time to share the ball, pass to others, cheer on the good shots from either team, and have fun while playing.

For those students and their families who want their child to play more competitively, I encourage them to seek out community sports. During these times at school, we let kids know that everyone has the right to participate and to be included in the game. Students can only get better with practice. If they don't ever get a chance to pass or kick the ball, how will they ever get better and increase their confidence? Yes, there are certainly other opportunities during physical education class, however the playing field is also a great place to start.

Childhood Trauma, Anxiety & Mental Health

Our Mental Health Depends on It

We have become more aware of the mental health crisis and certainly the explosive increase in anxiety, especially amongst our teens. We see the ability of our teen's resiliency weakening or becoming non-existent at an alarming speed.

Have you ever noticed that teens these days are reluctant to try new things or take risks? More often than not they say, "I can't" or "I won't" without even trying.

Let's be honest, our collective mental health is being taxed to the hilt! That's the bad news, the good news is as parents you can support your teen to help them manage to get through this together.

ACES aren't always winners!

ACEs in this particular case are not the winning hand in a card game, but rather *Adverse Childhood Experiences* which can pose problems in areas such as mental and physical health as well as the possibility of social issues throughout a person's life.

These experiences have been grouped into three categories, abuse, neglect, and family dysfunction before the age of 18, as determined by a study conducted by the Alberta Centre for Child, Family and Community Research.

As we have gained a better understanding of the developmental aspects of the brain over the past several years, it has been noted that toxic stress has detrimental effects on a growing and developing brain. These experiences make it ever more challenging for some young people to cope, including displaying limited resiliency skills, emotional regulation, and focus as a few examples.

- "People with three ACEs or more are more likely to use drugs at an early age, have a teenage pregnancy, develop a drug or alcohol addiction, or marry someone with an alcohol addiction. They are also more likely to have a lifetime history of depression or attempt suicide. Liver disease, heart disease, stroke, diabetes, chronic lung disease, chronic pain and irritable bowel syndrome are also linked to ACEs."

Here are a few examples to help explain ACEs courtesy of APPLEmag.ca:

- "An adult in a child's home makes verbal insults or threats
- An adult physically abuses (injures or bruises) a child in their home
- An adult or someone five or more years older makes inappropriate sexual advances to or contact with a child
- A child sees her mother or stepmother being treated violently (pushed, grabbed, slapped, had something thrown at her, kicked, bitten, hit)
- Someone in the child's home abuses alcohol or drugs, is depressed or mentally ill, or has a disability that limits or interferes with daily activities
- A child is often bullied
- A child often feels unloved, afraid or isolated
- A child's parents separate or divorce"

It is interesting to state that many of us have experienced ACEs in our young lives, and it is important to provide stable and supportive relationships early in a child's life in order for the impact of these experiences to be diminished. Knowing and understanding about the experiences and providing professional guidance can support your teen in establishing strategies, strength of character, resiliency, and determination to create a strong and healthy lifestyle as they mature. Left untreated, the results could be devastating.

Not My Kid

In conversations with parents I have heard this repeatedly; parents often say that "they don't understand what is going on with their child."

"I've never seen this before; this doesn't happen at home."

"My son or daughter wouldn't act like that."

"I don't know how to engage with my kid."

"Something is happening with them, I'm worried."

"They've changed!"

I have often told parents that, yes, they really are your children, and they will be back.

Insert tiny chuckle (inside voice). This uncertainty, aloofness, independence, rude, crude, and socially unacceptable attitude, language, and behavior are generally the most noticeable. Teens are trying to figure things out, be independent, pretend that you don't know what you are talking about, pretend that you don't matter, all the while they are oftentimes afraid to ask you and sometimes, they just don't know what to say or how to say it, but they sure do hope that you are there for them anyway. These times provide you with the opportunity to ask questions differently, to be curiously engaged and to have those Courageous Conversations that might be difficult for you and for them. The questions or open-ended statements that you say need to be intentional without seeming like you are prying, even when you are. Your ears must be vessels of pure listening compassion, your heart open and loving, without judgment.

When I was growing up, I heard many disparaging and hateful words in my home, and it made me feel unsafe to share about my relationship, especially when I was dating a person of another color and I was refused, by my father, to continue to have relations with that person. I never shared about my interest and attraction to women. Both of those examples were heartbreaking to me because they were about me, the importance of my personal relationships was threatened and not acknowledged by my parents. As a result, I could never celebrate or ever discuss my personal life with them until well into my later adult years. Only then did we start to have Courageous Conversations. It was a sense of relief, even though so much time had passed, the loneliness of not being able to share the intimacies of my life with my parents was very sad for me. The disconnect was palpable, even as I share this with you now.

Teens are seeking acknowledgement, and they want an opportunity to have and use their voice. They want you to answer their questions, or at least suggest where they might find an answer, and go with them. They want you to tell them that it's ok, to listen to their concerns, their fears, and their goals for the future. The enormity of their feelings and worries gets in the way of them seeing what is possible. Can you relate? How easy is it for you to get sidetracked with worry and fear, not believing that you can make a difference in your own life or even your family's lives? The number of times that I have heard,

"It'll be easier when I'm gone."
"I can't take it anymore."
"I'm nothing or nobody."
"It feels so hopeless."

The pain and anguish on a child's face and in their heart is soul crushing and heartbreaking. We need to be able to say, "I've got you, no matter what!" Unfortunately, that doesn't happen as often as we would hope.

Those are some of the concerns that are present right now. Those are some of the reasons kids are cutting, that's why they are thinking about and, in some unfortunate cases, actually completing suicide because they don't see that there is hope for them. They don't see anyone out there who is ready to support them and be their champion in this life. If it's not you, who will it be?

SAFETY AND OUR MINDSET -
how anxiety shows up

The brain and the body respond to stress in a variety of ways to protect itself, more specifically, us. Its focus is on protecting us both consciously and subconsciously. We typically respond with fight, flight or freeze. Let's take this a bit deeper with this illustration; if you were to meet a ferocious bear on a pathway, your body and brain would likely do one of the following:

FIGHT: Stay and take on the bear, NOT LIKELY. It would include self-preservation.

FLIGHT: Other than knowing that it's not the best idea to run away from a bear, they do run quite fast, your brain and body are likely responding in that fashion. Let's get the hell out of here and now!!!

FREEZE: Your brain and body go into a panic state, and nothing functions normally, panic sets in, everything in your body is paralyzed.

These same responses are elicited in our body when other situations occur as well, whether the issue or concern is life threatening or when someone is scheduled to visit the dentist, speak in front of a group of people or when someone is asked a question when they have been caught off guard. This can even happen when teachers ask a student questions, and the student then feels embarrassed or afraid to respond in front of their peers. This is a good time to inquire as to what is under the surface of their response. Having a conversation with your teen and inquiring as to what is making them respond in the way that they do. Being curiously engaged and asking questions can provide a safe space because you are asking the question without judgment.

"You have mentioned that you hate it when the teacher asks you a question. When the teacher asks you a question, how does it make you feel? What are some of the things that you think about? What happens in your body?"

Prompting along the way can help provide more information for your teen.

"Do you get nervous? What does that look like or feel like in your body?" Don't expect an immediate response, because oftentimes teens don't understand their emotions and it takes time for them to process their feelings.

"Could it be fear of not knowing the correct answer? Was it that you felt singled out? Was the teacher just looking for a general response and mentioned your name to get your attention?" the parent asks. The purpose of asking is to understand and provide support for your teen to take a risk by taking action, either in the class or in trying on a new activity that might scare them.

Understand that everyone at some time in their lives is afraid, and they take the appropriate steps to conquer their fear by placing one foot in front of the other and moving through the challenge in front of them. As their parent, checking in with them will help to reduce the anxiety and assist them in understanding that it is seldom about being called out, but rather a moment in time when the teacher is verifying that the student understands so that they can help with the issue or concern or acknowledge a job well done.

You could ask questions like,

"What is the worst that could happen if the teacher asks a question, and you don't know the answer or your work isn't complete? Could you ask for an extension or some assistance? Would that be the end of the world?" These questions will help with clarity and understanding. We often conjure up the most incredible stories in our head about what might happen, only to find out that our fear driven thoughts are holding us back from speaking, attempting something new or really accomplishing a task, activity or taking a risk. Often, the accomplishment is far greater than the actual fear.

Inclusion - The Gift of Soulful Understanding

What happens if your son or daughter is gay or if they declare that they are transgender? Would you give up on your child if he or she came out to you? If your daughter was pregnant or your son told you that he was going to be a father. In trying to find his way, you find out that your son is in a gang or that your daughter is dealing drugs and working in the sex trade. Your child is in a relationship with a person of another culture, race, religion etc. How do you see yourself responding?

These are questions and considerations that require you to dig deeply into your own soul and heart space and answer those questions for yourself. What do you do? How do you work through this with your teen? They need to know that you care and that you love them, no matter what. Be careful not to diminish their sharing. It takes a great deal of courage and bravery to be able to tell you their story. They want your love and understanding more than anything.

If they've heard disparaging words around your house with regards to someone's sexual orientation or race or other language that is disrespectful to others, they will not be inclined to tell you what's on their heart. What are you going do about it? How are you going to be able to support your teen if you have an attitude or behavior that's different from what they need? What they are seeking for themselves is someone to be strong, supportive, loving and someone who will care for them, no matter what. If they don't see it from you, then they don't have you to turn to. Perhaps they have other people at school, possibly sharing with their friends, or they could be alone in their struggle to figure things out. They very well could be targeted at school as well, what then? If you are lucky, they will continue to search for a teacher, counselor or someone whom they hope can do something for them, someone who will guide and support them with respect and honor. If they are unlucky, you may find your child turning to drugs, unsavory street activity, cutting, and other self-harm activities or attempts to end their life because they don't see any other alternative. This is often the time when they start seeking approval, and it might not be with the most appropriate groups. Keep in mind that a gang is a family as well. Not likely what you had in mind, but that misguided connection occurs more frequently than you would imagine as an outlet, albeit not the smartest or safest.

Inclusion and Diversity

Your child befriends a new student named Arun; his family is of refugee status. They are new immigrants to our magnificent country. Arun does not have full command of the English language and add that to a young person's already heavy backpack of trauma and violence that they had been through or witnessed prior to arriving at your teen's school. What a challenging beginning. They too can feel the pressure, anxiety, heartbreak, despair, loneliness, depression, guilt, and shame of what they have experienced and are grateful for this new opportunity to create a better life.

Your teen wants to invite Arun to come over to your house to meet you and hang out. You tell your teen some half-truth about why you don't think they should play or hang out with this other child. Meanwhile you are wielding your own fears and misunderstandings about who that child or family is. Your own bias, hatred, fear, prejudice, racism comes flowing out with no regard for the health and well-being of your own child. Why can't they have this friend? What's stopping you from showing up for your teen in a different way, to break through your own fear and misinformation?

Let me remind you of the bigotry, hatred, prejudice, and hateful rhetoric that is hitting the news these days. It's certainly not new; however, now it is out of the darkness and into the light. How do you support your child if you have these underlying views? Your new modeling could be the breakthrough that your child needs to see to help them learn to be open and welcoming to others. Will you continue to perpetuate your viewpoint, or will you provide them a gateway to a new way of thinking that provides space for inclusion rather than isolation?

What am I really trying to share with you? Give yourself permission to not know everything and begin to have new courageous conversations with your child. Become curiously engaged and open to different perspectives, especially those of your child.

Here are a few more examples to use:

"I noticed in the school newsletter that your class sizes have increased. You must have lots of new students in your class?"

"Have you introduced yourself to anyone new in your class?"

"Have you volunteered to take them around the school and introduce them to your friends?"

"It must be very scary to start in a new school without knowing anyone. What do you think it might be like?"

"Imagine if that was you? What would you want someone to do for you as you start in a new school?"

If you have noticed changes in your child's demeanor you could try:

"What's it like for you in school when . . . ?"

"I notice that you are looking or feeling . . . What's going on?"

Try to identify the type of emotion that you think your child is demonstrating, using it in your description. If they agree, that's great . . . if they don't agree and they tell you "That's not it" either try another 'feeling' word or ask them to explain further. Helping them to identify what's happening and how they are feeling is really important and will help them heal faster.

This language may be a bit strange or somewhat awkward at first, try it on anyway. Help your child to know that you are trying to understand where they are coming from. An expression of your own bottled-up emotion shared with your child can begin to help them know that you are safe to be with, so that they can share with you. This is not a quick fix, it's the beginning of a new relationship forming with you and your teen. Give it time, be patient, work through it with them.

Holding Space for Strong Emotions

You likely have the ability to recognize your own emotions, and you know how to deal with them most of the time. Even if you hold onto an emotion and let it spill out into other areas of your life, you have the knowledge and the tools to 'make it right' when you make a mistake. For example, if you get angry with your teen, you can admit that you sometimes get angry with them. You can also share that it isn't always about them, but rather something that happened at work or elsewhere that you didn't deal with the situation appropriately and were afraid to have a courageous conversation with your co-worker. You have the ability to explain the impact of not dealing with the situation and showing your teen the possible results of that impact.

"I took it out on you when I came home today, and I apologize. I shouldn't have said that to you or responded in that way. I had a challenging day and I'm frustrated that I didn't deal with it at work like I should have. You got my frustration, and it wasn't even your fault," you explain. "You see how that can happen when you don't deal with issues when they arise? Sometimes in anger we say things that are hurtful and it's necessary to use the 24-hour rule, which means not responding right away to an email or a phone call that makes you upset, but rather taking the time to think about it, understand the other person's perspective and leave it alone until the next day. It usually diminishes the intensity of anger or frustration. Because if you answer with your own anger in the email or the phone call, it generally doesn't go well, and you say things that you cannot take back. Including what happened with you and I, when I walked in the door angry from a situation and you got the anger, instead of my leaving it at the door."

Continue to listen for their response because your child or children do have a voice. Helping them learn how to deal with your emotions in a respectful and responsible way helps them learn how to deal with their own.

Teenagers feel strong emotions, just like we do. Here is how you can help them explore the plethora of feelings your teen may experience.

- Be curiously engaged and ask questions for an understanding of how your child is feeling.
- Ask them to describe as best as they can.
- When you have that feeling in your body, where do you feel it most?
- In what part of your body is it located?
- Describe the feeling.
- When did this feeling start?
- How do you think it started?

Providing a few examples or prompts will usually help to get the information you need; however, it's important to be careful not to answer the question for them, this is their experience. Give your teen time to reflect for themselves, time to process and gather their thoughts. This should not be a time when you are filling the space with conversation. Silence is okay and can be helpful. Tone and a dismissive attitude can also be cause for alarm with a teen who is trying to process their feelings. Avoid the tendency to diminish thoughts and feelings by saying things like "Oh, don't be silly, it's not like that" or "Don't worry about it". Understand that these are their thoughts and feelings, and they are difficult enough to process without you invalidating them or unintentionally dismissing them.

Guilt. Can best be described as having committed a breach of conduct according to the Merriam-Webster Dictionary definition.

What can we do about it?

Recognize that your child might not necessarily be able to identify the feeling that they are experiencing. It is important to teach the young person about 'guilt'. It may or may not be an emotion that comes to mind readily or is even understood fully.

How do we recognize guilt?

It is usually displayed as a feeling of remorse for some wrong act or deed, something that they did wrong, whether it is real or imagined in their mind.

You could say, "Remember the time when you did (or said) this _____ and you said you were sorry? What made you say that you were sorry?" Let your teen think and respond, then continue to help them understand the concept of guilt.

How do we eliminate guilt from our lives or at least recognize and deal with it when it arises?

Depending on how wrapped up your child becomes in their worry or guilt, and whether we overcompensate or overreact with our own feelings of stress and anxiety about the issue or concern, will determine how we need to proceed to help them understand. Guilt can be managed with your reasonable and responsible decision-making skills and abilities which, as you know, need to be modeled and taught in order to have your young person fully understand and demonstrate at future times for themselves and with others.

Remorse: Can best be described as having a sense of guilt from something that they did in the past.

Does everyone feel remorse? No, unfortunately, many people don't feel a sense of remorse for an action or inaction. Some people cannot recognize beyond themselves that when a 'wrong' hurt whether by words or action was committed, they cannot recognize the impact on the person harmed. Often, it has to be fully explained in order for that person to understand the impact of their action or words. "When you said _____, it really hurt my feelings."

How do we teach it?

First, when we feel remorse we need to model it, explain when a situation occurs, and how and why expressing remorse it is important. Then explain how to recognize it and how we should respond to it. You could ask,

"If someone swore at or tried to hurt your family members, say mom or dad or one of your siblings, how would you want that person to respond to your family member? Would

146

you want them to be sorry for their actions? If that person were honestly sorry about how they hurt your family member or even you, that would be remorse. They were sorry for what they had said or done and took the time to say they were sorry. Not just saying the words, but really displaying an honest response to their hurtful action, as well as recognizing that they shouldn't do that hurtful act again." The importance of this is also to share with your teen that the word 'sorry' is thrown around too easily and without regard for the feelings of another. The real purpose of saying sorry is to change our behavior and try not to repeat that action or say those words. It defeats the purpose of saying 'sorry' if the action is never altered or it is repeated without reflection.

Shame: Merriam-Webster Dictionary defines shame as:

- A painful emotion caused by consciousness of guilt.
- Short coming or impropriety.
- A feeling of inferiority.
- The perception of oneself as a failure or feel unacceptable to others.
- Flawed, unworthy, not good enough.

People who are put down or insulted as children, either directly or indirectly, end up much more prone to 'shame-based thinking' as adults.

> "Shame is not helpful or productive. It can be a source of destructive, hurtful, and unhealthy behavior. Believing that we are flawed, unworthy of love and belonging makes us unworthy of connection." *Brené Brown*

As a result, we believe that we are not important or of value to anyone including ourselves. In teenagers, these feelings can often lead to self-harm and suicidal ideation with the result being suicide. Based on statistics from the Canadian Mental Health Association and Statistics Canada, acceleration into harmful situations is becoming more prevalent amongst teens and young adults. This is evidenced by the fact that there has been a 60% increase in hospitalizations for mental disorders among youth between the periods of 2008-2009 and 2018-2019, and suicide is the second leading cause of death among those aged 15 to 34 years of age.

Chapter 6 Recap

- Parent asks "Hey, I was reading an article today about this child who was abused by her neighbor. My heart was breaking thinking about you. If something like that happened to you or say a friend of yours, what would you do about it? Would you tell me so that we could help you through it? If it happened to you, would you feel that you could come to me to tell me about it? I understand that it would be very difficult to share, and you wouldn't want to tell me - I do want to know so that we can work through this together."

- Bring 'neutral' into your commentary about your ex-partner so that your child doesn't feel trapped between the two of you. Help them to know and understand what's important in a healthy relationship. They only see you and your relationship as the model.

- Trauma can be different for everyone. Be gentle in your understanding with yourself and your teen while working through it.

- Social Isolation: Are you part of encouraging it with your constant engagement with your cell phone or being too busy?

- Is cell phone use functional or dysfunctional in your home?

- Helping your child up after a fall is far more powerful than never letting them fall.

- Is the argument really worth the pain that it causes? How could you reframe your thoughts and feelings so that they are heard, understood, and valued?

Call to Action

> ➤ Make a plan with your family to have "cell free" time (time away from your phones).
> ➤ Play a game together, go on a walk or hike, go buy ice cream (without using your phone).
> ➤ Have a meal together at least once a week, "no cell phone" zone.
> ➤ Monitor the cell phones regularly.
> ➤ Create 'rules of use' together.
> ➤ Make a plan of where the cell phones sleep at night.

Chapter 7
Stop Bullying, Start Loving

. . . it's everyone's concern. . . WE need to Be the Change. . .

Bullying is at epic proportions! It has affected many of us in some fashion throughout our lives. As we see it in our daily lives, on media outlets, intimidation and harassment are common in our places of business, our neighborhoods, sporting and social events, our country, our political arenas and in our world as demonstrated with global political and social unrest.

I often hear that "schools are doing nothing".

"There's so much bullying in my child's school,"

"My child gets bullied every day and nobody is doing anything about it."

Bullying is most commonly defined as repetitive, purposeful and deliberate physical, emotional, and/or psychological aggression which may also include harassment and violence. The unfortunate thing is that everything gets lumped and dumped into the term "bullying."

"Mommy, she looked at me during class and gave me a mean look."

"He budged me," (jumped in line in front of me).

"She took the ball when it wasn't her turn."

"They talked about me behind my back."

It lands clearly on the shoulders of schools and educators and the expectation that it should be our responsibility alone to make bullying end. The thing I find the most fascinating is that we don't teach bullying in school. More often we are teaching positive values, morals, ethics and leadership skills that enhance a child's development and provide them with foundational skills that can be nurtured and developed throughout their life. In some jurisdictions we are teaching religious beliefs, how to be safe and caring, stranger danger and other significant skills. Steven Covey's Leader in Me Schools, 7 Habits of Highly Effective Kids, PMAST (Peer Mediation and Skills Training), the Dare to Care program, MADD (Mothers Against Drunk Driving) and so many other exceptional programs exist and are part of many curricula in schools. All types of programs with the aim of supporting students to function properly within school and hopefully take these skills into the world.

One of the fundamental principles of these workshops and programs is that the key to making them work and have long-lasting effect is for them to be fully implemented in a teen-ager's life, and that includes in the home. Parental participation is critical to their success. Unfortunately, all too often, many of these programs have limited attendance when offered to parents to participate. The issue lies in the challenge to have parents attend these workshops to gain insight and encouraging them to work alongside the educators and their own children to help model appropriate behaviors. As adults, we may have had a taste of teasing, being made fun of or being part of teasing someone else. We were teased and relentlessly taunted because of how we looked, an unpleasant or downright nasty comment about our hair, our outfit, our size, our skin color, our boyfriend, girlfriend, because we might have been gay or not, the fact that we wore braces or glasses, we were tall, small, fat or skinny, too smart or a geek, stupid or a dumbass or just because someone felt like it. You may have given up on the prospect of being picked for a team or chosen for a part in a play because you were worried about the possible fallout and commentary. Unfounded rumors may have been your plight. Some of those behaviors may have even worked their way into your adult life. Any way you look at it, we've all been part of it, whether you were laughed at or did the laughing, standing around and watching or just walking away without doing anything. It's imperative that we become part of the solution so that we can make it stop! Where is our common decency and respect for one another? We need to be able to recognize the impact of our words and actions and demonstrate humility rather than humiliation!

Your Own Bullying Experiences

"I didn't really mean it . . ."

What is your earliest memory of being bullied, teased or made fun of? I want you to get really connected with your feelings. Where you were, what happened, who else was there? Staying with that feeling, notice where that feeling is in your body. How did it make you feel? What did you decide in that moment about how you would be? What would you do and who would you become? How old were you when this event happened to you?

I bet there was hesitation in even wanting to think about that time. You may still have some embarrassment around the situation, nervousness that travels through your body, shame, guilt, and countless other emotions that have come up for you. Did you notice how clearly and precisely you were able to recall the exact event and all of the minute details? You may also be saying, "I've diminished the thought", "That was a long time ago, I'm over it!" However, we do know that experiencing bullying in childhood can have profound effects on mental health in adulthood, and that can influence how we function, as adults: how we act, react and go through our lives. Somehow, we weren't able to bottle it up in our past as well as we thought we could because even with all these years since that event it keeps showing up, rearing its ugly head in our mind, actions, lives, work, play, and business affairs.

This is also what is happening with your children, these effects are in real time.

We now have TV shows that thrive on criticizing people in public. Shows like American Idol, Survivor or The Housewives series. If you scroll more frequently on social media, you are more likely to see clickbait headlines and algorithms that are skewed to negative emotions. The amusement and acknowledgement that shows and media get by their enormous ratings is really appalling; while innocent people are subjected to ridicule, and we think that the show or media events should be on more often. The more we berate people or make fun of them, the more people laugh - how frightening is that? Yet we allow it to continue. We seem to take great joy in the misgivings of others. From our playgrounds to our politicians and the wars in the world. Have we become so desensitized that it doesn't matter? Our common response is "Whatever, it doesn't affect me," and then you see how people are treated and how it does impact and affect them. There are so many children and adults who still feel the wrath of despair because of the bullying or teasing that they received or were part of during their daily lives.

It comes in many forms, in every walk of life, and in every age group. The senseless violence, verbal, physical, emotional, social, sexual, cyber aggression must be stopped in order for each of us to grow and develop into thriving human beings. It's never too late to learn compassion, empathy, caring, and kindness to create a safe and loving environment where peace reigns. It's not a 'pie in the sky' solution that is unattainable, it requires all of us to listen to and understand each other, to accept differences and work together. We are stronger together.

"What can you do to promote world peace? Go home and love your family." *Mother Teresa*

Bullying at School - Is That Where it Starts?

Your children spend many waking hours at school, oftentimes more than the number they spend at home with their families. School is a breeding ground of activity, sometimes misaligned, rough, physical, irrational, and immature. It is also a place to develop skills of cooperation, competition, resiliency, and an understanding of fair play. Often there is an imbalance of power either by size, strength, age, attitude, behavior (including mean and hurtful words), physical and emotional aggression, and unruly behavior. Aggressiveness often leading to fights, intimidation, threats, attacks, bodily injury and, in some cases, haunted to death resulting in children turning to cutting, alcohol, drug abuse, depression, and suicide.

I'm sure you are getting the picture!

> **Behavior is a form of communication,
> listen and watch closely.**

Emmanuel's Story

The hallways were bustling with students rushing off to their sessions of the Leadership Conference we were hosting in our school. The excitement was palpable. In this particular session students were encouraged to send texts to the speaker to ask questions or to provide information about their response to dealing with bullying.

The students who gathered in the library listened to the speaker share her own story of being bullied. She asked,

"Have any of you either been bullied or are bullies in this school?"

After a moment or two of absolute silence, Emmanuel slowly raised his hand and shared his experience about being picked on and bullied throughout each day.

"Students would bump into me at the lockers, it happened so often I finally asked Ms. Bennett if I could have a different locker away from those students. I was able to get a corner locker and that helped a bit. They often took my personal belongings, like my favorite hat, and they would toss it amongst their group, finding any way that they could to annoy and irritate me." He explained, "I felt like everybody hated me and I didn't want to come to school anymore. I tried really hard not to get angry and stay away from them, but it felt like it was happening in every class, and I was getting sick of it. I finally told my teachers about it, and they tried hard to help, but these kids just kept doing stuff when no one was looking. It was getting to the point that I just wanted to kill myself."

The room fell silent, some students lowered their heads, others looked around not quite knowing where to look or what to do. The speaker added her closing commentary with,

"Perhaps you are now aware of the impact of your actions and inaction when others are effected like this. I acknowledge you Emmanuel, for being so courageous in sharing your story. I'm sorry that this has happened to you. It shouldn't be happening to anybody. You are a powerful leader who is making a difference by using your voice and sharing your experiences. I'm certain that there are many more students right here who needed to hear your story so that they can change theirs."

Again, there was silence as the presenter was packing up her things. A few students in the group texted the speaker and commented that they had no idea that Emmanuel felt that way and they could see that their comments and teasing had had a terrible effect on him. Some students wrote notes of apology and positive affirmations to Emmanuel and gave them to him later in the day. That day many things changed!

The effects can be devastating and yet comments and situations like that and worse happen every day. Where do they come from and why are they necessary? It was a clear reminder of how easy it is to use words to be hurtful. We all need to be reminded that our words can be used as weapons or as healers for others.

Not all Bullies are Students

The office area was quiet as we had just finished morning announcements. I was approaching the office counter where one of our parents, Mrs. Mallard, was standing to say good morning. I overheard her speaking to the secretary saying,

"He's an idiot and useless, he wouldn't get it anyway," speaking about her own son in front of the office window. I was taken aback by what I was hearing. Her son Jaxon was standing right here. I opened the office door and was walking through it to address what I had just heard,

"Mrs. Mallard, do you have a moment?"

She responded, "I don't have time right now to chat, I'm running late for another appointment," as she turned away and pushed her way through the front door and out of the building.

I stood aghast. *What parent says that about their child?* rushing through my head. You are likely saying, "Oh, I'm sure she was kidding, she didn't mean it?" "REALLY?" *What part of that commentary was humorous?* I thought to myself. *Who in their right mind would say that? Especially with their child standing right there!* I saw the look on Jaxon's face as he walked away, certain in my mind that no part of that was fun for him. Unfortunately, that's probably the reason why he didn't engage very often in his work, with people in his class or with any activity. He would say and do inappropriate things to be accepted within his peer group. Understandable, however sad to say the least. He was often seen 'hanging back' because he didn't know where he fit in. I thought about letting him go to class and then I decided that I would speak with him and help lift his spirits, or, at best, reframe his thinking for a moment.

"Hey Jaxon, stop for a minute. Why don't you come back this way? I'd like to chat with you about something. Don't worry, you're not in trouble," as I smiled at him. As he came closer I asked, "I'm getting a glass of water, do you want one?"

"No thanks" he said.

"Are you sure?" I asked again, and he nodded yes. When I returned from the staff room, I handed Jaxon a glass I had filled for him. I pointed to the chairs in my office with my open hand and said, "Choose whichever one you want," as I closed the door to my office, walked over to my chair and sat down. "I heard what your mother said and I wanted to chat with her about it, but she said she had to go. I'm sorry that she said that to you. Please know that I don't think that way about you. I think you are a great kid and I want to help you do well while you are here. You only have a couple more years before you head to high school. So, let's try to make it a good time."

"She was only kidding," Jaxon said as he looked away, then lowered his head.

It sure didn't sound that way to me, I muttered to myself in my head.

"Tell me what's going on with you Jaxon. You've looked sad and depressed lately. What's been happening?"

"We just came back from the doctor, and he told me that I have type 1 diabetes. I don't know what it really means, and I don't know what to do."

"What did your mom say?" I inquired.

"My mother told me to just suck it up and follow the diet. Besides you need to lose weight anyway." Jaxon said.

Tears flowing down his face and not knowing where to look, he sat quietly. I grabbed the box of Kleenex and slid it over to where he was sitting. Jaxon grabbed one and wiped his eyes and blew his nose. I reached under my desk for the garbage can and lifted it up and he threw the little heap of tissue into the garbage, and I returned the garbage can to its place by my feet. He sat for a moment without saying anything with his eyes looking down and said,

"I don't have any friends; I just hang out with them here. I don't really like school and now this."

After a few more minutes of silence, he stood up from his seat and was moving towards the door when I told him, "We have a school nurse who comes every week. I can ask her to speak with you. She will have suggestions about how to support you and give you some ideas for meals and how to take control of this for yourself. What do you think, buddy? Want to give it a try?"

After a brief hesitation he looked up and said, "Yes, thanks."

"Great! I'll let her know. I think she's here this Thursday. Perhaps you two can talk then."

"Thanks Ms." Jaxon responded as he turned the knob on the door and opened it.

"I can also let Ms. Peters, our counselor know if you want and she can speak with you. You can leave her a note and let her know when you would like to chat with her. That would be up to you if you feel comfortable with that. Or if you like I could chat with her, and she could then make a plan with you to meet. What do you think? Can that work?" As I stood up from my desk. "Let me know if there is anything else that I can do to help you out, okay Jaxon?"

Jaxon turned his head toward me, "Sure."

Just as he was about to walk through the office I said, "I'll call and let your teacher know that you were with me." He nodded his head in acknowledgement as he left my office and shuffled his way down the hallway to class.

After I called his class and spoke with his teacher, I sat back down at my desk thinking about how many other kids have struggles going on in their life that we have absolutely no idea about, and they are carrying their heavy burdens all by themselves. Hurtful, destructive, sarcastic comments can really affect people, so much so that they don't step into their own greatness, whether child or adult, because they don't believe they can.

I still deal with it from time to time with the committee in my head that provides commentary "Who do you think you are? Look around, what do you have to offer? Who's going to listen to you?" I now have the skills to thank the committee for their opinion and contribution and I flick them off my shoulder and take steps toward action, no matter how small the step, it gets me closer to where I really want to be.

As adults we sometimes have more strategies, age, and experience to help ward off those feelings. If that is the case, how is it that we have so many folks who hide using drugs, alcohol, shopping, gambling, those who suffer from mental distress, who cut or worst of all take their own life? It comes because they think that they are of no worth or value, they have no purpose or feeling like they are not capable of making a difference in the world, for their family, friends or themselves. What a terrible burden that is! We still hold onto that suitcase, the heavy backpack, straight jacket or ball and chain that we are dragging around with us or however you want to imagine it. We hold onto the past, with our limiting beliefs showing up every day staring us in the face and we create our lives based on those old feelings. How limiting is that? However, even more tragic, what does happen is that we dump those old limiting beliefs and all our own personal guilt, shame, hurt, and fear on those around us.

Now let's look at our children who have had far fewer years on this planet, and they are supposed to know and act and do the right thing, behave in a certain way and control their emotions. How do they do it when they might be dysregulated or in other words, don't have their emotional shit together? What are they learning, as illustrated by the story of the mother and her disparaging words to her son? Not all bullies are fellow students, sometimes they are siblings or parents that do the most harm.

Some of our children are incredibly resilient and others, not so much!

> **The missing pieces are connection, courageous conversations and love . . . no matter what!**

How to Explore Bullying With Your Teen

From time to time we all need to be reminded that we will not get along with everyone we meet. It can be more inspiring to share with children that relationships can grow and develop when they are nourished and nurtured in order to keep them strong. Inquiring with your teen or young person about what they are seeing and hearing when having issues within their classes or on the playground. Continue to be curiously engaged by asking questions like:

"When you say that you see that student or friend looking at you, what makes you feel that they are angry or upset with you?"

"How do you know that they feel that way? Did you talk with them about it?"

"What gives you that impression? What are you making it mean when. . ." This question is really important as it provides an opportunity for your teen to really think about what's going on for them that is causing them to feel that way about the other person. Does your teen also need to be responsible for their own actions in that relationship with the other person? Something to consider and inquire with your teen. Are they perhaps not being completely honest in their response? This again is not a blame game, but rather a chance for them to understand the impact of their actions in a relationship. Taking the time to explain that assuming we think we know what the other person is thinking or feeling, guessing at their facial expressions without checking it out, we then make up stories in our head about what we believe to be true.

We get infuriated parents who come stomping into school and say, "MY KID IS BEING BULLIED AND WHAT ARE YOU GOING TO DO ABOUT IT?" Standing over the teacher or administrator, typically and figuratively, pointing and yelling. I wonder why that child might possibly be a victim or actually be a bully to others?

What we currently have are layers of dysfunction demonstrated, perhaps at home and in the community, with sarcasm, jokes, put-downs, teasing, fighting, name calling, physical aggression and so much more. Have you been in a hockey arena or a soccer pitch lately while teens are playing? We wonder why kids have become so aggressive in sports and on their playgrounds. The name calling, verbal abuse and harassment that come spewing from fans in the stands is absolutely despicable. In the school setting, I have often witnessed and certainly been part of the interaction with parents and teachers. Parents are often afraid to talk with their child's teachers because of how they feel based on an experience as an adult or as a child in their own personal life. They feel intimidated because they don't know enough, they weren't good at school, and the list goes on!

The teacher, meanwhile, is worried about the terrible reaction a parent could have during a conversation about their child's classroom occurrences. For example, John's not doing his homework or Katherine is not attentive in class which creates the need for a conversation or a meeting with a parent and the teacher. The power imbalance shows up and no one is able to deal with the issue of the child because they are both fighting with their own inner demons. Teachers can sometimes be positional; feeling that they too have the right answer and know better. It's important for parents to know that they can ask for an administrator to be present for their meeting. This typically helps to assure that both sides have the opportunity to share their viewpoint and are really heard. Administrators do their best to balance the information and assist each side in reaching a common ground and an equitable solution. Interestingly enough, the imbalance and the intimidating attitude and behavior sometimes come from the parent. The teacher could be experiencing a similar feeling based on something that might have happened to them in their own school experiences or worrying about the terrible reaction a parent might have. The parent says that her child doesn't do well in that subject, say math as an example, and comments that they didn't do well or hated math, and therefore it should be ok that their child doesn't need to work on it. *"Are you kidding me?" as I shake my head.* Then you can imagine the challenge for the teacher.

From time to time the situation is then ramped up, emotions elevate amongst the adults and the situation doesn't really get addressed in the way that either party hoped it would. It becomes the "blame game" with no one really taking responsibility for their own actions. Just a reminder, this is what our children see, particularly if they have attended the parent and teacher meeting. Did it help to resolve the situation? This is a tiny glimpse as to what it is like from the school perspective.

If you are angry about something, then demonstrate it in a way that is a positive model for your child(ren). If they don't have that positive modeling, then they won't know how to act reasonably and responsibly in situations when something might make them angry. How will they deal with it? This is where you muster up your courage, address the issue, demonstrate or model an appropriate manner, and explain how to work through the issue. If they continue to see poor or inappropriate behavior from you, it's no wonder they act in a similar fashion at school or on the playground, athletics, with other members of your family or even with you.

If something happens in your family like the death of a loved one, including animals, loss of a job, hearing about a friend or family member who has been struck by tragedy or illness, it's important to let them see you hurt, sad, devastated, crying, depressed, and be able to talk with them about it. That's what helps your child to be resilient, understanding, empathic, and caring. Seeing you struggle, show your emotions, take the time to work through it, and have conversations with your kids, again demonstrates and provides them the opportunity for learning and growing into a caring and compassionate adult. When we don't take the time to share, be vulnerable, have these Courageous Conversations, we set up our children for avoidance, unstable relationships with their friends and eventual partners, who they will most likely pretend with as well and say that everything is "OK" when it's not!

When children can't show emotion to someone they care about, and they don't have the opportunity to get in touch with their own emotions and feelings, it leaves them unavailable to others in commitment and positive attachment.

It is important to be aware that our thoughts and background aren't necessarily the same as our children's perspective, which oftentimes creates anxiety in them and in us. We are not our parents; however, oftentimes we show up sounding and acting just like them. Do you often find yourself saying something to your kids that your mom or dad said to you?

This is a great time to ask your child the question 'What are you making it mean?'

"When you said that Melissa looked at you with a mean look today in class, what did you make that mean?"

It assists in having the Courageous Conversation about what they are thinking and feeling about a particular incident or situation. Using this question gives your child an opportunity to explain how they were feeling or what was going on in their mind about the situation. What's their perspective? Check in with your child, really understand what's going on under their words. Feelings about hearing 'You just need to work harder' or 'I'm not good enough' could be lingering in the background of your child's mind. Ask whether you are supposed to just listen 'without judgment,' providing your commentary, or do they want a different perspective and advice, or possibly a solution to the situation? This might provide an opportunity for you to be a sounding board and actively listening rather than only giving solutions. Provide space for frustration, anger, sadness, guilt, and any other emotion that might be bubbling up within your child. It creates the start for new ways of being with each other. These questions that you use and work through with your child can also be questions that your child uses for themselves when and if a situation occurs at school or in the community. 'What am I making it mean?' This very powerful question can be used to de-escalate the possibility of a fight, misunderstanding or hurt feelings.

In a previous chapter we took a step into where you child might be learning these types of behaviors. In reflection, you took time and looked a little deeper and investigated for yourself, what are the possible places that my child might be exposed to these behaviors or are these behaviors somehow being modeled for them, by me?

Let's look at some of the skills, strategies, and knowledge that would be worthwhile to share with young people and teens, as well as what we might very well have to remind ourselves about as we journey every day. We hear through our own filters, which means that we have a way of seeing the world through our own experiences, our past and how it has shaped us to see the world. It's now time to try to see and understand the story of another through a different perspective, without saying "That's not so" or "It's not like that." I get it, it's in your background, your upbringing, the filter that you hear through, see and live through. To really connect, you need to be able to take on another's worldview. Remember, it's the other person's perspective from their life experiences, not yours.

My mother and I were having tea at her kitchen table, and she asked me,

"So how are things going?'

"I'm so excited about my new business, working with parents and their children. However, I have so many stories of heartbreak and sadness when it comes to talking with parents about issues like conflict and bullying. I want to do so much more to help people realize that what we need is understanding, love, and compassion for each other. That doesn't cost anything. Right now, it's costing people their lives and that needs to stop. For God's sake, why can't we just get along!" I explained to my mother.

As she was adding sugar and stirring the tea in her mug, she pulled in her chair a little closer to the table and sat down. She smiled a faint smile in acknowledgement and then her facial expression changed quite seriously as she frowned and paused. Looking at her cup with her head down she said,

"When I first came to Canada and started school I tried to follow along as best as I could. Trying my best to keep up with my new work and do what I was told. I recall that we were doing math and the teacher had asked if anyone hadn't finished their work, and he told us to come to his desk. I thought that he was going to help and show us how to complete the work because I wasn't quite sure how to complete it, some of it was quite new to me. As you know, I was quite shy, so I didn't really want to ask anyone for help. I didn't want to bother him or any of the other students. As the other students rose to move, I just stood and followed a few of them and arrived at the teacher's desk. The teacher instructed us to hold out our hand, one on top of the other," my mother demonstrated to me as she was telling her story. "Pulling the drawer of his desk open and taking out a long piece of leather, he proceeded to give each of us the strap for not having completed our work." As my mother shared the story, you could see the emotion that had welled up in her and the tears in her eyes. She continued, "I recall the students who sat beside me stood up and told the teacher that I was new to the class and was not entirely familiar with the work. Unfortunately, the teacher had already extolled the virtue of his power."

I share this example as an illustration of how we hold onto our feelings, situations, and memories as if they had just occurred. My mother also explained,

"What I realized in my life was that it had held me back from wanting to try new things or embarking on new adventures. The fear became overwhelming, and it took over my life." At the time of telling her story, she was 87.

The sharing of this information is so that we can all take an active role in eliminating bullying in our schools, our homes, our workplaces, our communities, and our world.

We have only touched the surface of dealing with bullying. The programs that have been administered by teachers have not really reached the intended audience, that being the rest of us. It cannot just be a program, presentation or lecture on how not to bully. A complete change of attitude and behavior about how we should treat each other has to be in the mix through education at school, in our homes, and our communities. When we focus on positive relationships, starting with looking at ourselves and moving outward from there, we can share those learnings with our teens. We really need to appreciate ourselves for our individual gifts and talents, our insecurities and forgive ourselves for taking everything so personally. When we are working from the inside out, we can begin to understand others and accept them for who they are. As we continue on this journey, we will begin to open up our courageous communication and conversations with others, that in the past may not have been possible. The relationship we develop within our families, our friends, interactions with our schools and community partners can help us work together to create an atmosphere of safety, connectedness, and a more positive culture of acceptance and tolerance, cultivating peace and forgiveness. We need to start somewhere!

Our world is broken, and we are in definite need of a change! This senseless violence must stop in order for our children to grow and develop into compassionate and caring adults in a safe and loving environment. Our own personal health and welfare depend on it. We can no longer sit by and complain about what is happening; it is up to us to believe in ourselves and the lives of others around us and not put up with the hurtful chatter, mindless and senseless humiliation, threatening attitudes and behaviors or the cruel and unusual personal punishment that we have accepted as a normal way of life. We have become complacent and desensitized to the degree of harm that bullying causes. It hurts to the core of our being, on a physical, psychological, social, emotional, and spiritual level.

It's quite fascinating that even as a bully, a person can recognize that their behavior had an impact and they feel remorse. Take my friend Valerie, for example. I had gone for a visit, and we were sitting out on her back deck sipping wine and looking at the magnificent view of the lake when she asked me,

"How are things going these days?" She knew that I was just starting this new business working with families, and as I was about to tell her what the latest was, she interrupted by saying, "I was a bully at school. I used to wait for this kid, I can't even remember his name, oh wait, it was Liam. Every opportunity I got, I would bump into him, knock his books out of his hands, do whatever I could to make his life miserable. What I discovered as an adult, as I thought about my behavior, I recognized for myself that it had been about my mother, and how controlling she was of me and my sister. I needed to regain my own control, so I took it out on other kids. I wish I knew where he was now because I could tell him how sorry I am for how stupid I was in reacting to him that way." Normally, a smiling and glee filled expression was on her face, that day it was replaced with a look of remorse and guilt. After a few minutes of silence, she commented, "I wish you luck with your business. It will help to change people's attitude and behavior. Yup, it's really needed in the world right now, it's out of control."

Voices Matter and We are Making Change

Often, we believe that we don't have a voice or that what we want to do doesn't matter, but it does. We have clear evidence to prove it in our daily lives. We have spoken up and people have listened. Look at what the latest fights for our lives have resulted in. We never imagined that smoking would be banned in public places, fighting against large multinational companies who ruled the industrialized world with billions of dollars in support of organizations, while at the same time killing or maiming millions of people while they puffed casually on cigarettes. We have been able to successfully push back the restrictions on smoking, and the sale of cigarettes have been a benefit to us. We can sit in a restaurant without breathing in the poisonous air of someone else smoking, we can fly in an airplane without the musty, stale smell of the smoker near us.

We now are reducing the number of plastic bags that we as consumers use to carry our purchases from the store because we have said "no" to pollution and turned our view to recycling in order to save our planet. We recycle, reuse, and compost like never before!

We have begun to change our choices for focus on a healthy lifestyle regarding the food choices that we make, our exercise programs, health and welfare in our workplace, making more healthful choices with medicine and natural choices.

Black Lives Matter, and the atrocities and the historic maltreatment of people of color, the racism within our professions, white supremacy and it's cancerous and insidious threat to our collective wellbeing. These morally destructive actions have now been brought into the light, albeit only after significant tragedy. My point being, that we have a voice that is no longer silent and hidden, but rather one that is shared with humanity in order to make change and declare that we are here on purpose, to live fulfilling lives and to make a difference.

So, what is stopping us from protecting ourselves and each other from the escalation of bullying around us? We see it in our homes, playgrounds, hockey rinks, soccer fields, schools, workplaces, and our governments. Are we going to just sit by and say that is how it is and has always been, or are we going to stand up and make a difference for ourselves, our children and our world? We must take action now; our lives and the lives of our loved ones lie in the balance!

> *Empathy:* The action of understanding, being aware of, being sensitive to, the experience of feelings or perspective of another person

Empathy

Empathy is a wonderful gift that is available to all of us. How do we teach our children and each other about it? Perhaps one of the best ways is to coach your young person or teen to be positive, resilient, powerful leaders now and into the future. Showing your children empathy and helping them to understand the nuances and diversity that is part of our world. Your work as parents is paramount to the change, strength and support that is required. Teaching them empathy is important because, you see, none of us are born with empathy, knowing or understanding kindness, we need to guide and nurture those traits and values. It's important to model and talk with your children and teach them how to be kind, caring, and empathic human beings. However, what we need to keep in mind is that you might not have empathy in your toolkit either. You might not have had positive examples of empathy, kindness or even caring in your life or in your background. So, demonstrating it to another person may be quite difficult.

The premise of empathy is to understand another person's perspective and being able to step into their shoes, see through their eyes, how they feel. It might not be your way of thinking; however, it helps to understand another person, their feelings and their concerns. Teachers may be able to demonstrate and talk about these values, but who better to model them than YOU! You can tell your child that it is new for you as well and that you can both go on that discovery together.

Empathy pulls people together while **sympathy** pulls people apart, cleverly described by Brené Brown in her YouTube video, *Brené Brown on Empathy vs Sympathy*. Empathy provides a place of understanding, listening, being there with another person. Sympathy is feeling sorry for someone. It does not provide an opening for understanding or compassion, it simply adds to the misery. You can provide the space for your teen to share their specific concern, issues, observations, tragedy or fear, without judgment, solution or the projection of our own feelings tossed into the mix. It has been referred to as "being with" someone. And, just for the record, empathy can be taught, even as an adult.

We need to help our teens discover who they are. We can help them to understand and become resilient, while not doing it for them or protecting them from everything, but rather by guiding them to know and to understand. This is also an aspect of empathy, being in another's shoes. When you teach and model, your child will learn how they will grow to be independent in their acting and thinking.

A question you might ask is, "What do you see in this situation that works and doesn't work? What other solution do you see possible?" We can't assume that we are going to get along with everyone and your teen might need to be reminded about that. Relationships grow and develop when they are nourished. Your engagement with your teen could also include helping them to understand and become critical thinkers, not someone who just follows along because their friend thought it was a good idea or they don't feel that they have a voice. Acknowledgement and support are really important as part of the connection. This acknowledgment, by way of encouragement and courageous conversation, also provides a trust and safety that your teen can experience that provides a space to work through with emotions such as stress, anxiety, fear, depression or not seeing the light as they stumble through the darkness. Nurturing their independence and providing them with the strength and skills to help them "turn on the light." This is also a time to encourage them to be risk takers. Taking gradual small risks, like you have done, provide them the strength to build the capacity to take on greater risks. This could be learning a new activity, a new language, jumping out of a plane, starting a business or becoming an entrepreneur. They will want and need to know that you are walking alongside them on their journey.

We have racial, cultural, religious, gender equality, disenfranchised, marginalized people and human rights concerns, as well as mental health, poverty and food concerns present in our society. Any of these issues would be a great starting point for your Courageous Conversation, while demonstrating how empathy works towards understanding. Many of these world issues will be areas that might also be of interest to your teen, with regards to making a change in the world and putting an end to suffering. You never know where the conversation and action might lead. It's an investment in our youth and for their future!

Forgiveness

A story that is my checkpoint for forgiveness for others was an incident that happened quite a number of years ago in Taber, Alberta. A student walked into his high school and began firing his sawed-off .22 caliber semiautomatic rifle at the students in the halls and cafeteria. One student was wounded, and another was shot and killed. A short time after the incident, the murdered child's father forgave the young man who had committed the heinous crime. Although the man was a pastor in his community, I was still shocked and dismayed by the brutal violence and wondered *How could he do that? How could he lose a son, his own flesh and blood, and be able to forgive this other human being for this terrible tragedy?* That was the questioning I did. I had to really search withing myself and fully understand the depth of love and forgiveness this man demonstrated to this other boy and to the boy's family as well. The father saw beneath the crime, he understood the turmoil that this young man was facing within himself, and he forgave. This unparalleled love and understanding were far stronger than the thought of action or revenge.

The point here is that the father did not condone the actions of this crime but identified the fear, depression, and isolation that were present to drive the young man to that action. As was also shared in the media, this killer had suffered severe bullying throughout his school years.

Can you look in places within your life where it's now the time to forgive? It is often not the action, but the underlying behavior, hurt, pain, and anguish that is yelling out for help. Unfortunately, they are often demonstrated through the terrible and often irreversible actions that we take, the hurt that we have within that we wield at others to escape from our own pain, that cause the real damage. Isn't it time to start to forgive in your own life?

Forgiveness is quite a complex action that we aren't really used to identifying. We say we are sorry for something; however, usually to someone, sorry is not forgiveness. You said sorry because you accidentally bumped into someone. Sorry means that you are going to change your behavior and make every effort not to repeat that action again. We use this word so haphazardly, with no real consideration or intention to change.

A definition (Wikipedia) of forgiveness can be best described as an intentional and voluntary process whereby the victim undergoes a change of feelings and attitude towards the offense and overcomes negative emotions such as resentment and vengeance. It can also include understanding the incident that happened, what you made it mean and letting it go. If you intentionally decide that you are forgiving someone, then you can't ever bring up the event again in conversation or in anger. Each time you do that, you give the incident more energy and you haven't really forgiven the other person. As truly challenging and difficult you might find this, you need to take some time to step into the other person's shoes, really look through their eyes, and see what was going on for them. I get that you might say, "What does that have to do with anything?" Keep in mind that they are a human being as well, with thoughts and feelings that might have been damaged in their life. Stay with me for a few more minutes in this place. See the world from their perspective. I'm reminding you that this is not condoning their behavior, but simply recognizing that it might not have truly been what they wanted to do, perhaps something snapped within them.

What makes forgiveness so complex is you need to be able to forgive yourself for taking the incident so personally. You need to forgive yourself for holding onto the hurt, frustration and anger within yourself because it will only cause you harm and pain. The resistance to letting it go will manifest in your body because now it is not only anger, pain, frustration; it builds to resentment, apathy, indifference, sadness and turmoil that lives only within your body. These feelings start manifesting within your cells and your body systems and they become the "dis – ease" (disease) that starts to show up in you, physically, mentally, and emotionally. When we get the full impact of truly forgiving someone, it shifts our emotional and physiological chemistry such that it releases those 'good for you' hormones that help us function in a more calm, peaceful, and mindful way. Understanding and sharing this information with your teen and helping them work through the challenges and responses that typically arise like, "I hate that person and I will not forgive them, they hurt me."

Here's where the Courageous Conversation can be set into motion, as you listen and agree that your child was in fact hurt and acknowledging the pain that they feel by using their words, it will then lead into you helping them to understand the other person's perspective. It is not to rationalize, but to explain that oftentimes 'hurt people' hurt people so that they can get away from their own pain. The forgiveness piece is to allow your child to rid themselves of the burden of holding onto the pain they have received and to free that other person, the one who inflicted the pain, from a power hold on your child's feelings. Once your child begins to understand the difference between resentment and true forgiveness, it becomes easier in time for your child to really let go of the pain and move to a more vibrant and alive place of their own. This brings us back to supporting our youth with their resilience so that they feel empowered to help themselves or others if bullying situations arise.

> *The village that it takes to raise a child needs to start with the family.* Elizabeth Bennett

Chapter 7 Recap

- Limiting beliefs keep us from moving forward. What is it that makes them so attractive to you?
- Getting uncomfortable is a sign of forward progress.
- Trauma can be the looking glass that helps us into a better place.
- Every triumph or failure will establish as a new and stronger bond in your relationship with your teen. It's what you are both looking for!
- You've found your connection, now make it yours!
- Recognizing the impact of our action and inaction is paramount to creating a safe and more peaceful environment. Wouldn't that be worth it for your family?
- Words can be weapons, or they can be words of wisdom and healing. Choose wisely!
- Different questions bring forth different answers - try different conversation starters.
- Stand in someone else's shoes, look through their eyes and imagine what it must be like to be them.
- Voices matter - let's use yours to change the world. . . for the better!

Call to Action

Often, parents are unaware if their child is really involved with bullying behavior. Was their child actually the bully, the person being harmed or the person who just stood by and watched the incident unfold and didn't engage, was too afraid or just walked away because it didn't involve them directly? To get a better idea of how teens think about bullying, you will find a collection of questions that you can use to have courageous conversations with your child. Oftentimes we don't really know what our teens think and what they want to do about it. What are their own personal thoughts and feelings? What are their fears with regards to bullying?

When reading through, you will find that some of these questions are direct and powerful while other questions are provided so that you can be curiously and seriously engaged in understanding what happens in school and the community, and what perspectives students take with regards to bullying. Some of their answers will surprise you and some will need further explanation both from them and from you. Be careful not to use too many of your own examples, use your dedicated listening skills to evaluate what they are saying, what you are hearing, and asking for confirmation in your understanding of what they are explaining. It's helpful to ask for examples when you are having these conversations so that the picture becomes clearer for understanding. I will also mention that this is only one perspective, and many sides of the story are required to obtain the larger picture. These are wonderful teaching moments that you can have with your teen. This is also a perfect time for them to begin to understand about other perspectives and the impact that bullying has on everyone.

- ➢ What does it look like in your class when someone gets teased or bullied?
- ➢ Does anyone make an effort to stop the person who is saying the mean things?
- ➢ Why do you suppose this happens in your class or on the field at lunch or after school?
- ➢ How do you contribute to bullying at school?
- ➢ When you see it happen, how do you respond?
- ➢ Are you sometimes just a bystander who watches while someone gets picked on?
- ➢ Does it occur to you that someone may need your help?
- ➢ Do you use your voice to stop the situation and call someone out?

➢ Do you simply walk away and let whatever happens, happen?

➢ If you were being bullied, would you hope that someone would stick up for you either by stepping in or getting a supervisor?

➢ Do you stand up to bullies or do you stand behind them and let them make others feel bad, or worse, get hurt?

➢ What are suggestions that you have to break the cycle of bullying in school?

➢ Why do you suppose bullying happens?

➢ Can you give me an example of something that you have seen and why you think it happened?

Here's What We Know For Sure

There has been a lot to digest here. We know that you are already an amazing parent who wants the connection with your teen, and you are willing to try and do anything to establish it and make it work. A variety of strategies, ideas and perspectives have been provided for you to tailor to your needs as you have courageous conversations with your teen.

The secret is *consistency* - trying out different strategies and seeing how they work. If one works today, keep in mind that it may not work tomorrow. Don't give up! Keep working on it with them. The harder it is, the more worthwhile it will be when you break through the barriers and have a powerful, connected relationship with your teen.

You don't need to be a perfect parent to make a connection. Your teen needs to see the real you, the vulnerable, the broken, the amazing you!

Every failure or triumph, whether it's yours or your teen's, will establish a new connection with a powerful sense of accomplishment, through caring, loving, and understanding.

You've got this!

177

AFTER THOUGHTS

- Our brain creates new neural pathways when we try new ideas, strategies, and when we understand different perspectives; the more we practice these new skills and strategies, the stronger our brain connections become, forming new habits.
- We don't have to parent like we were parented.
- Do you recall being permissive as a child or as an adult? How did it make you feel? How do you think others around you felt? Safe, secure, loved, accepted?
- Do you recall being domineering as a child or as an adult? How did it make your feel? How do you think others around you felt? Safe, secure, loved, accepted?
- Come alongside: create new connections and relationships with your teen and your family.
- Forgiveness: forgive yourself for taking things so personally. Forgive others freely - why carry around old anger, resentment and hurt? (It's only hurting you).
- Life pressures, expectations, stress, anxiety, worries ~ Breathe.
- Complex emotions: anger, sadness, fear, guilt, shame, unworthiness, jealousy, rage, grief . . . acknowledge these emotions, don't let them rule you or your loved ones.

- Unmet needs hidden under emotion: feelings unexpressed, held back, unpredictable - these can cause conflict at home, with partners, family, friends or work. Be vulnerable, talk through them with courage.
- Acknowledge the emotions - what are the unmet needs?
- Guidance and direction: do you have a clear direction and are you ready to guide?
- Be responsible: for your actions or inaction, they both have a result - opportunity or consequence? Your choice.
- What is needed to make it all work?
- What perspective are you taking, and can it be shifted?
- Are you mirroring your own parents' ways of being?
- Feelings and needs matter!
- Parents don't always know how to ask questions, you might feel like you are prying. . . how will you know what is going on if you don't ask questions and get curiously engaged?
- Rigid thought process: "You weren't raised that way! Be seen and not heard." Now is the time to break free from that way of thinking.
- Parents feel isolated. Teens feel isolated.
- Let's try a new approach - help teach and guide yourself and your child.
- Children need to be seen and heard and have their needs met.
- Parents are sacrificing so much to provide for their children - that creates a model for children that isn't always the best (too busy to feel, engage, hear or listen, share or be there). How will you make that different?

- Teens and young people require guidance, rules, and boundaries so that there are clear expectations for everyone - have conversations with understanding and love at the centre.

Courageous Conversations require:
- ➤ Cooperation
- ➤ Valuing everyone and their perspectives
- ➤ Acknowledging feelings
- ➤ Engaging the Five Strategies of Dedicated Listening

For more information, please visit my website:
https://www.elizabethbennettgroup.com

ACKNOWLEDGEMENTS

I'd like to thank the thousands of students and their parents whom I have had the absolute blessing to have worked and played with each day of my career. I am grateful to all of you. Especially to those with whom I have laughed and cried, fought through challenges and walked alongside; each of you have taught me so much. You have helped me to become a soulful teacher and a passionate leader. It has truly changed my life!

I want to thank my parents. I know Dad, that you are looking down at me from heaven with a twinkle in your eye and pride for this and many other of my accomplishments. To my mother, I thank you for your constant support and amazing love. You both provided the beginning of the roadmap for my journey to where it has led me today. Although bumpy at times, and certainly not without pain, sorrow, and joy, I'm grateful for the genes of determination and persistence which I inherited from both of you. I have learned that in order to succeed in life I must be willing to do whatever it takes to heal and move forward, growing with each lesson. My fiery attitude and heart-centered desire also come from you and for that I am incredibly grateful.

To my writing coach, Tammy Plunkett, it has been an absolutely incredible journey and I am truly grateful for the opportunity to have worked with you on this writing project. Your skillful ability to hold my feet to the fire, to get me to keep going, and the masterful way you have encouraged me has been astounding. Have you started editing my newest writing yet? It's a detective novel, you know. Soon to be a 'made for TV movie'. (A Netflix original). I'm excited to have you work on that one next!

Thanks to the team members of our mastermind writing group. Your support, encouragement and helpful tidbits of information have helped to keep me moving along. It's been a pleasure to hear about your individual writing journeys and the accomplishments that lie ahead as a result of a job well done. Looking forward to reading your works of art!

To my business mentor and friend, Michelle Nedelec. Your behind-the-scenes encouragement and enthusiasm for my work has been the candle that has lit the way. Thank you for always being there for me.

Gratitude and love to my partner, Heather, who has been with me along this journey to the accomplishment of this project. Her support and encouragement have been a blessing.

I want to thank Connie Jakab, the members of the Brave Parent Institute, and the Flourishing Parents group who encouraged and supported my efforts. You are all amazing gifts to your families and the world.

To so many others who have encouraged me along the way, I appreciate and love you all.

This has been an incredible journey. I never imagined in my wildest dreams that this would actually be something that I could accomplish. Imagine me, a best-selling author of my own book!
Joyful blessings,
Elizabeth

REFERENCES

Alberta Family Wellness Initiative. 2018. "Our brain thrives on connections" Our Brain Your Guide (page 14), apple.
Alberta Family Wellness Initiative. 2018. "When ACEs are too high" Our Brain Your Guide (page 26), apple. https://www.applemag-digital.com/applemag/our_brain_2018?pg=1#pg1

Brown, Brené. 2013. "Shame vs Guilt" brenebrown.com. January 15, 2013. https://brenebrown.com/articles/2013/01/15/shame-v-guilt/

Canadian Mental Health Association. 2021. "Fast Facts about Mental Health and Mental Illness". CMHA National. July 19, 2021. https://cmha.ca/brochure/fast-facts-about-mental-illness/

Casey,B.J., Rebecca M. Jones, and Todd A. Hare. 2008. "The Adolescent Brain" National Center for Biotechnology Information. March 2008. https://www.ncbi.nlm.nih.gov/pmc/articles/PMC2475802/

Bronson Gray, Barbara. 2012. "Teens Benefit by Spending More Time With Parents" MedicineNet. August 21, 2012. https://www.medicinenet.com/script/main/art.asp?articlekey=161620.

Greene, Ross W. 2016. "Lost and Found: Helping Behaviorally Challenging Students (And, While You're At It, All The Others)" Jossey-Bass.

Leaf, Caroline. 2021. "Cleaning up Your Mental Mess: 5 Simple, Scientifically Proven Steps to Reduce Anxiety, Stress, and Toxic Thinking" Baker Books, a division of Baker Publishing Group. https://www.drleaf.com

Association for Psychological Science, 2011. "Social Acceptance and Rejection: The Sweet and the Bitter." August 12, 2011. https://www.psychologicalscience.org/news/releases/social-acceptance-and-rejection-the-sweet-and-the-bitter.html

Chirban, John T. 2014. "Appearance and Peer Pressure" Psychology Today. March 30, 2014. https://www.psychologytoday.com/us/blog/age-un-innocence/201403/appearance-and-peer-pressure

Psychology Today. "Forgiveness" https://www.psychologytoday.com/intl/basics/forgiveness

Siegel, Daniel. 2014. "How the Teen Brain Transforms Relationships" Greater Good Magazine, August 12, 2014. https://greatergood.berkeley.edu/article/item/how_the_teen_brain_transforms_relationships

Siegel, Daniel and Tina Payne Bryson PhD, 2011. "The Whole-Brain Child: 12 Revolutionary Strategies to Nurture Your Child's Developing Mind" Bantam.

Statistics Canada, 2020. "Suicide in Canada: Key Statistics (Infographic)" The Government of Canada, Last Modified March 4, 2020. https://www.canada.ca/en/public-health/services/publications/healthy-living/suicide-canada-key-statistics-infographic.html

TED. "Rita Pierson: *Every kid needs a champion*" YouTube video, 00:07:48. May 3, 2013. https://www.youtube.com/watch?v=SFnMTHhKdkw

CPSIA information can be obtained
at www.ICGtesting.com
Printed in the USA
BVHW031209150323
660239BV00001B/5

9 781778 266508